SET FREE YOUR
Flow

A CENTERED VIEW

Selin Senol Akin

A CENTERED VIEW

Copyright ©2021 SELIN SENOL-AKIN

All Rights Reserved

No part of this book may be reproduced, or stored in a retrieval system, or transmitted in any form or by any means, electronic, mechanical, photocopying, recording, or otherwise, without express written permission of the publisher, except in the case of brief quotations embodied in critical reviews and certain other noncommercial uses permitted by copyright law.

ISBN: 9781734656350

Author Photography by: Dayanch Kakabayev

PRINTED IN THE UNITED STATES OF AMERICA

SET FREE YOUR FLOW

*To my daughter, Dalya,
and all free spirits
attempting emancipation
from cultural chains
that clash with the creativity in their veins:*

May you always feel content in your inherent flow and identity

A CENTERED VIEW

she made me do it
my divided soul
the one I cannot control

for when, using logic, I try to do so;
she shatters, like glass ensuing freefall
and I ultimately risk losing it all

so here I go,
I unleash her truth
as I best know
the urban and the floral
the liberal and the moral

I set free her flow
perhaps, thus, we can
finally heal and grow

SET FREE YOUR FLOW

to be lost
in the **flow**
in that focused moment of
creativity

your artistry
and authenticity
safe and sound

no need to be found
no disillusioning distractions
that make your heart pound

to soar the world
in mind and spirit
with both feet
firmly on the ground

"The happiest people spend much time in a state of *flow*- the state in which people are so involved in an activity that nothing else seems to matter; the experience itself is so enjoyable that people will do it even at great cost, for the sheer sake of doing it."

"To overcome the anxieties and depressions of contemporary life, individuals must become independent of the social environment to the degree that they no longer respond exclusively in terms of its rewards and punishments. To achieve such autonomy, a person has to learn to provide rewards to his/herself. He/she has to develop the ability to find enjoyment and purpose *regardless of external circumstances.*"

— **Mihaly Csikszentmihalyi,** ***Flow: The Psychology of Optimal Experience***

A CENTERED VIEW

Dear Reader

Yes, you. If this collection has found its way to you, then I believe you too to somehow have felt at one point to be in the eye of the storm called *identity*. Smack in the middle: *centered* between right and left. Geographically. Ideologically. At times attempting to mediate between the two forces. At others: to be 'centered' and 'aware' enough to actively enjoy being in the present, rather than constantly reflect on the past or future. Admittedly, I have only been able to do both through biographical self-analysis in retrospect, and sometimes still face the same struggles I will delve into here in this collection.

According to the late social psychologist Peter Weinreich:

"A person's identity is defined as the totality of one's self-construal, in which how one construes oneself in the present expresses the continuity between how one construes oneself as one was in the past and how one construes oneself as one aspires to be in the future…One's *ethnic identity* is defined as that part of the totality of one's self-construal made up of those dimensions that express the continuity between one's construal of past ancestry and one's future aspirations in relation to ethnicity…"

(*Theories of Race and Ethnic Relations*. Comparative Ethnic and Race Relations. Cambridge: Cambridge University Press. 1988)

SET FREE YOUR FLOW

What makes you *you*? And What makes me *me*?

Splendid literature has been written by bi-cultural authors (mostly vis-à-vis their biracialism in particular), discussing the difficulty of a *dichotomous* life a character experiences while growing up.

But these are *my* drops. My autobiographical 'contribution' into the bucket of human collective stories forming global oceans: akin to what psychologists have called a 'global consciousness'.

And who am I?

No one special. No one with any mission other than being a storyteller. A voice for the less-frequently voiced, if even at all.

General details of my childhood are known by those who know me in real life. Some are also known by my likely-annoyed language students, for I've repeatedly shared with them biographical anecdotes in an effort to motivate them whenever I sensed the confidence in their language prowess begin to dim. Most frequently, I've relayed my 'Storytelling Contest' representation of the public school I attended in the 4th grade, just one year after immigrating to the United States with my mother.

In retrospect, I would consider this my first sense of 'accomplishment' in this country, as well as a 'catalyst' sign intended for eventually dedicating my life to becoming a

A CENTERED VIEW

storyteller.

My subjective 'drop' of storytelling to pour into that 'global consciousness' of human interconnectedness (addressed mostly in my premier poetic collection, *Write Out Your Drops*) has been a little bit of many things. In Turkish, we have a coinage: *'ortaya karışık'*. It roughly translates to 'a little bit of everything mixed together in the middle', and is mostly used to order a variety of appetizers in restaurants (If you've never ordered eggplant appetizers at a Mediterranean restaurant, you don't know what you're missing).

'Ortaya karışık'. That's exactly how I felt growing up as an *Istanbulite* child in New York City: smack in the 'center' of various dichotomies. East and West. Villager and Urbanite. Traditional and Modern. Politically correct and political outcast. The family pleaser and the black sheep.

Through my musings, I attempt to not only provide you with *a view from the middle* (my first intended definition of 'a centered view'), but also increase my own sense of balance and self-awareness ('centeredness') through self-reflection. And, in doing so, hopefully allow you to be able to do the same for your own *self*.

Empathetic reader. You will be reading the following short essays and poetic verses from a woman-child who was raised as a bi-cultural person in the United States. (I was raised here, yes, yet even at the age of nearly 37 as I write this: I'm not sure whether or not I've yet grown up). An overly-sensitive woman, as well as an empath to other people's pain- who's been let down countlessly with the expectation that such sensitivity would be returned to me. I've been called 'childish' many times and by many people: with both good-natured intentions in using that word, and bad.

By blood I am Turkish, and by cultural-upbringing: an American. I am equally Turkish and American. I am equally East and West. (Some pan-European Turks would argue that Turkish culture isn't very representative of the East, but I'm a realist who begs to differ. I'm of the view that while geographically and ethnically Turkey is most certainly Eurasian, many of its cultural expectations and customs have more in common with the 'East'). And I strive every day simply for balance: grateful to be alive.

In theater, middle rows and 'center' seats are often favored: they're an easier-on-the-eyes 'view' of the performance. You can view the main event on stage from all sides, from different vantage points. I write now my own such view.

It was the great Shakespeare, wasn't it- who said that the world is a 'stage' and that we are all merely 'the players'? What if we're more so the *audience*, observing natural events and how all living thing go about fulfilling the various necessities for survival- albeit from different angles in accordance with our world views and social identifications? I've come to follow various animals in my backyard lately;

sparrows have built a nest in one corner of our roof, for example, while a showier male cardinal in his red glory chirps every morning alone. From my 'view from the middle' of both a liberal and traditional perspective, I imagine the birds in the nest as having built a traditional home as a family, while the cardinal chirps alone in a melancholy tone. The cardinal searches, I imagine, for a home or at least a partner of his own with whom to roam. 'The Settled' versus 'The Vagabond', I title them. Whenever I view them, I smirk.

I was raised smack in the middle of the storm where East and West would often clash, just like my dreams. I've now come, however, to not only accept my bicultural identity (which I'd spent my entire life running from, in order to 'fit in' better just in one category) but actually to be empowered by my duality. I feel this has allowed me to become more 'centered' and present in the here and now, without being ashamed of my past, nor worried about the future.

I hope this personal overview of what has 'catalyzed' me into becoming the teacher and author that I am today makes you smile. Regardless of your background: if you can relate at all, and feel inspired even a teensy bit? Well then, my various 'drops' to ultimately form these 'collectively-oceanic' flowing waters will have been worth it. My nickname growing up, 'Sel', after all, translates to a 'flood'.

SET FREE YOUR FLOW

With *Write Out Your Drops*, drops of sweat from my struggles and the drops of emotional tears I shed created a waterfall. With this collection, I aim to create an over*flow* of individuality *blowing* through people's souls- winds that aren't filtered by cultural expectations and limitations. So that we may create hurricanes of a better kind than the destructive one of nature: hurricanes of art and authenticity so strong that dogma cannot diminish them.

I thank you in advance for allowing the ramblings of my consciousness and memories into your precious reading time and mental space. I hope my 'centered view' of self-knowledge and cultural observations allow you to *set free your own flow.*

XOXO

Selin Senol Akin

A CENTERED VIEW

TABLE OF CONTENTS

flowing through the veins: *Lineal Legacy*
pg. 15

flowing through relationships: *Imperfect Empath*
pg. 53

flowing through socialization: *Extraverted Introvert*
pg. 90

flowing through parenting: *Poetic Politics*
pg. 124

flowing through creating: *Lion in the Cat's Reflection*
pg. 172

SECTION I: Flowing Through the Veins

LINEAL LEGACY

A CENTERED VIEW

who can hold your hand,
when you cannot extend it?

why you have to be a storm, to thrive and keep warm
they'll never comprehend it

juggling two worlds
palms full
heart wary

you're dual, in one individual
and two can become heavy
for the soul to carry

delicate balance,
indecision and responsibility

your vulnerability
bare
let them judge
if they dare

tears flood your soul
whilst you feign not to care

SET FREE YOUR FLOW

ESTEEM

how enchanting
it would have been
to be transported to times gone by
merely through a wish,
or touching historic marble

then again- we can do so, can we not?

old neighborhoods
old loves
old joys and smells
old flaws

causing nostalgic retrograde

we're all living legends
to someone or other on this earth
realize your value and worth

before you are merely like that stone

immortalized
long after you can
recognize

A CENTERED VIEW

Books Over Looks

When you tell a fellow Turk you're from the historically popular city 'Istanbul', they often follow up with, 'how about your homeland- *memleket?*'
Istanbul, after all, is the Eastern twin of New York City- and I by no means believe it to have been random coincidence that I was meant to have been raised as an equal part of both places.

In my family's case, we could be considered relatively 'original' Istanbulites, I suppose. Istanbul is where my grandparents emigrated to from their native Bulgarian city of Plovdiv, following Communist repression of Muslims in the early 1950's.

It's funny. My 'duality' had begun before I ever moved to the United States with my mother at nearly age 8. Long before becoming a Turkish-American citizen, I had frequently felt torn between the often-discussed 'two different Turkeys' in my home country of Türkiye: the 'secularist' and the 'traditional'.

I'll never forget walking in a relatively 'conservative' part of Istanbul one day as a young child holding my mother's hand, and hearing a little boy around my age call to his headscarf-covered mother: "Look mommy, wh*res are passing by…"

Now, I'm happy to say that Turkey has come a long way since the early 1990's in regards to the mutual acceptance of and friendship between Muslim women choosing to cover their hair and those who don't. But at the time- and, especially as a little girl who didn't even fully understand the degrading term in Turkish- I was shocked. Not only by the boy's verbal outburst at my mother- who'd just been dressed casually in jeans and a baggy t-shirt- but by the random action in itself.

What must have that little boy heard about 'uncovered' women at home in order to so casually have made such a remark, as if pointing out to his mother some zebras at a zoo? Furthermore, what must have become of that little boy, I wonder, as a man now around my age?

Has he been able to evolve from such flawed thinking stemming from his childhood, or, sadly- gone to mistreat and judgingly-label more women in his subsequent life?

This recognition of there being a socially-perceived 'dichotomy' between two types of women in Turkey began, therefore, when I was a young girl in Turkey- and only escalated over time.

Whenever I met a Turk here in the United States who didn't seem to understand why I wasn't as 'excited' about our traditional cooking, holidays, and customs as they were- they often talked to me with judgement. Their words and looks in response to my indifference would almost always make me feel as if they were looking down on me, their attitude coming across as thinking, *'so you think you're too cool and Americanized for our customs now'*? But what they didn't get was this: even back in Turkey, I hadn't been raised to prioritize such customs, either.

My late grandmother, Emine, with her trendy two-piece suits, light green eyes and chestnut curls looking 'Hollywood' in photographs, began to cover her hair in her later years with a bonnet and prayed 5 times a day in accordance with the Koran.

My paternal grandmother, Hafize- equally lovely and an immigrant from Bulgaria herself- remains similarly pious to this day, wearing a more traditional headscarf. Yet this is where their similarities would end. Emine was a 'city girl' reared toward becoming a professional woman and kept her spiritual life mostly to herself, while Hafize went on to reproduce 5 children and lived mostly in a domesticated lifestyle. Both my late grandfathers- whom I remember for their warmth (Hasan, descending from Georgia and Ismet, from Bulgaria)- were never really the 'strict' types either. They both smoked cigarettes heavily, enjoyed convivial spirits in the home, and rarely went 'macho' on their spouses or offspring.

Perhaps, dear reader, even by birth and genetics, therefore, I was never from very typically 'traditional' roots. Perhaps if my biological father, Zafer (more on him in the next section), had chosen to remain in my life and I'd been raised with his family's influence rather than my mother's, I could have somewhat been more into Turkish holiday celebrations and various customs, as most of my cousins tend to be. But, alas, I wasn't. I was raised mostly by my mother and her small family. No big *Ramazan* celebrations. No encouraged hand-kissing of the elders. No baking something 'special' every week for 'big family dinners'. No observable 'Turkishness' aside from an inherent love of our cuisine, historical attractions and music, which remains to this day.

Perhaps this, perhaps that. Allow me, dear reader, to cut to the chase. Whatever 'Turkishness' I had learned as a young girl, I learned predominantly from my relatively more 'liberal', working/then-single mother (I was never around my relatively more traditional set of grandparents geographically). But, of course, Turks I met growing up in New York couldn't have known that. They'd view me as 'snobby' or somehow as 'forcibly westernizing' myself each time I expressed disinterest in Turkish customs. In reality: I simply wasn't familiar, and had never felt an inherent (or environmentally-enforced) inclination towards such traditions.

My 'centered view' is thus, quite literally, from the middle of not only Turkish and American cultures, but also a traditional and liberal worldview in general.

While I aim to express my unique view, I cannot ever state, in fairness, that I was distinctly 'torn' between my mother's 'eastern' ways and the relatively more 'western' ones of my Americanized upbringing (with my Turkish-American stepdad, and more on him a litter later as well). In hindsight, in fact, I can now hypothesize that the two parents who've influenced me were equally torn between the 'right' and 'left' themselves!

While one parent clearly was more center-right while the other was more center-left- relatively speaking- I was never directly pressured or reprimanded by my mother or stepdad for having chosen any one side over the other in my decision-making.

My bicultural duality and dichotomous struggles were caused more so by my own self-identity and image; by how I never felt able to` 'fit in' among any of the social circles I'd frequent. I didn't want to disappoint anyone- and hence often ended up disappointing myself.

My mother, stepfather, as well as many friends growing up would themselves often experience feeling torn between a stern mindset and an open one. The definition of 'strength' whenever I'd hear her name- my mother, Aysu- for example, didn't lead a traditional lifestyle, yes, but her mindset certainly was as such.

SET FREE YOUR FLOW

She'd grown up among a repressed yet curious generation in Turkey that had unknowingly planted the seeds of the dichotomy many of us as their children being born in the 1970's and 1980's would face. I'd even go so far as to liken Turkey's cultural dichotomy to the neighboring Persian one- with the only difference really being our secular laws contrasting with their theocratical ones. Like the character Nassrin of the renowned Azar Nafisi novel, *Reading Lolita in Tehran,* describes: knowing "…what it means to be caught between tradition and change (having always) been in the middle of it…"

Even in our native Istanbul- trendy clothes and discotheques would scream 'West', while ultimately becoming silenced with the daily calls to prayer from mosque minarets. My mother wanted to see me become a 'career woman', yes, but never make love to a man I wasn't married to. She and many other similar mothers of her generation would expect their children- especially daughters- to remain virgins even if marriage had to be delayed until well into one's 30's to be able to advance professionally.

My maternal grandmother continuously praised feminist-leaning ideals and never implied to me that a woman's main role was purely based on domesticity and marriage. 'My granddaughter is going to be a doctor,' she would fantasize in the letters she'd written to me after we moved to New York.

A CENTERED VIEW

(Sorry, *anneanneciğim*. I haven't become a doctor. But I am an academic. I hope that can still make your spirit smile somehow. In Turkish, both professions are, after all, addressed as *Hocam*).

My mother, her matriarchal heir, took such feminist ideals up a notch. My books always took precedence over my looks. In fact, whenever a family friend told my mother I was 'pretty'. she'd brush it off with that dreaded Turkish sarcasm *çirkin kızım benim* ('my ugly daughter'), in order to avoid that other cornerstone of Turkishness- *nazar* ('evil eye'). Whenever someone would suggest marriage, she'd tell them, half-jokingly, that I was still momentarily 'married to my books'.

My life status was preached to be elevated through self-advancement, not purely through marriage or customary feminine 'roles'. My late grandmother witnessed war. My mother witnessed her marriage crumble by infidelity and betrayal. They were both working women interested more in earned respect and social status than perfecting or promoting their traditional parsley and cheese pies- *börek*. (I'm not exaggerating. Most Turkish women- young or old- are somehow always pressured to preach something they cook or bake especially well. 'Oh, whoever marries our Ayşe will be lucky- her baklava is spectacular!')

And there I was- reared to develop my 'Turkish-feminine' identity through traits somewhere between those of the two women; *always smack in the middle* of something or other. Just like the time I was sitting- literally- between my late grandmother and my mother on a Turkish Airlines flight from New York to Istanbul. My mom had been relishing in the pride of a daughter having shown her mother the 'new world' for the first time in a 'look ma I've made it' moment. And that flight happened to make it onto the Turkish newspaper the following day for falling in the air for about a good 10 seconds during severe turbulence.

There I was. Seated 'smack' in between them- my grandmother of the stern exterior and romantic, musical interior (she'd sing like a canary about heartbreak every time I saw her), and my heartbroken-about-men mother. And we were all praying and holding one another's hands as we were lifted up in our seats during the freefall (despite the seat belts), imagining our end and praying for some sort of familial reunion on 'the other side' after the pending doom.

The pilot luckily regained control and the plane didn't crush anything except my sense of bravery on any flight ever since (I still redden with panic attacks and repeat every Islamic prayer I ever memorized in my head at the slightest turbulence).

I liken myself sometimes to the main character in the popular children's tale *Goldilocks and the Three Little Bears.* You know, Goldilocks- the girl who prefers the porridge, bed, as well as the seat of the youngest bear for being 'not too hot/cold, not too big/small, not too hard/soft, but in the *middle* as being 'just right'.

The things I've lived through have felt 'not too traditional' but 'not too liberal', either. Though I grew up feeling in limbo over the difficulty of choosing or appeasing one 'side' or the other, I've now- at nearly 37- come to welcome the nostalgia of having experienced 'a little bit of both worlds'. This fuels my inner need to empower others through my particular vantage point's storytelling, in fact. I can empathize with people from traditional backgrounds, as well as liberal ones. I can empathize with a myriad of minority groups struggling to 'belong' in certain settings: black or white, hijabi or non-hijabi, gay or straight.

Life is beautiful, but full of so many challenges already: economic, romantic, professional. So when 'social' categorization enters the mix- if you don't feel like you 'fit in' to live 'freely' as the flow of your soul dictates you to- you cry rivers while projecting rainbow smiles. The 'flow' inside me begs not to forcefully blow to 'sway' readers in any particular direction, but rather to be the 'wind' beneath their wings and behind their sails, aiding them along in their own journeys.

SET FREE YOUR FLOW

Before I end this portion of my prose, I cannot avoid one other elephant in the room- namely, the political one. But before I get to the international one that's trapped my daughter's innocent father behind bars later on in the book, I'd like to start with a snippet from my domestic experience with politics.

I was a former intern at both the Clinton Global Initiative and the United Nations. In fact, I was-what I'd deemed- a 'professional intern' for years after graduate school. Like many things in my life, my life was looking 'good on paper' to our Turkish-American social circle, though I wasn't getting much personal satisfaction, professional progress or financial benefit of any kind.

Most recently, right around the time when the pandemic first hit, I'd had the 'redirection' (I don't believe in empowering the word 'misfortune' by labeling it as such) of not only having my first novel 'The Catalyst' be published during such a timing, but, encouraged by local registered Democrats, running for local office in the primaries of my local Electoral District in Queens.

During the quarantine, with less opportunities for face-to-face interaction while attempting to obtain the required signatures from my neighbors to even be on the ballot for the basic/immediate-neighborhood-blocks-representing position, I was only able to end up receiving about one third of the vote. I lost to a neighbor I was curious to never see campaigning, until

A CENTERED VIEW

the mystery became solved when I later found out she'd had 'connections' and was a 'top-down' appointee who didn't exactly need to hustle like I did.

At the same time, I'm also someone who's voted for a Republican or two before, citing some policies- especially foreign- with which I agreed more. Why aren't I, then, registered as an Independent, you may ask? Metaphorically, yes, I suppose that would have been more befitting. As someone suffering from something I'll call *bicultural neurosis*- that mental struggle of tottering between 'am I fulfilling my full potential?' versus 'am I bringing honor to my family?'- I have often felt disturbed, in fact, by the American electoral system of having to choose between two polarized political parties, for any realistic poll victory. The reality that as an 'Independent', a candidate I support, or, heck, even myself at the local level would have no real chance for any position with teeth, 'catalyzed' me, I suppose, in choosing one side once and for all.

I could never say, 'Screw Turkish customs, mom- I'm American, and 18, so I'll be moving out now and you can't interfere in my decisions' (No such Hallmark-movie moments for this one here). I also could not only never say 'Screw Westernization'—which, in this globalized day and age, would be hard for almost any young person in the world to do anyway- but also never 'screw American individualism and idealism'.

SET FREE YOUR FLOW

I wanted my individualistic dreams to come true, but also somehow be able to form a home where Turkish food and music was welcome. Whenever I would try to have both, circumstances would always somehow leave me to fend for myself alone- and I could never quite muster up the courage to lose the benefits of both. I have a poem in my premier poetic collection- *Write Out Your Drops*- entitled 'Mata Hari' about this. "World War 3 exists every season, between my heart, body, and sense of reason," it begins. "...When I cannot choose, I am often imprisoned for treason," it ends. Indeed, I observed that when we couldn't 'choose', it'd truly feel like we 'lose' in life.

So, I eventually learned to dim the fire I felt for both, projecting a lukewarm sense of comfort in the two cultures instead. In my opinion, because I couldn't choose just one side to fully 'live out' and 'set free' in my bicultural identity, I felt empowered in the forced decision to choose one political party to support and run under.

Political parties haven't been the only dilemma. The choice of a soccer team- a huge deal among Turks everywhere that has even been known to ruin friendships if you support 'the other side' in any crucial match- has also always felt troubling.

I was raised as a supporter of *Galatasaray*, for example, having been influenced by my dear late uncle Aydın, with whom I even attended a major game against our archrival '*Fenerbahçe*' in their home-base of Kadıköy, Istanbul. As someone from Kadıköy (who not only would stay there during summer vacations but also lived there to teach English on her own for a few years as an adult), I felt socially tormented by not supporting the team all my local friends had been supporting so adamantly, including a guy I was dating at the time. Luck would have it that later I'd end up marrying a fervent supporter of neither Galatasaray or Fenerbahçe, but of the 'third' major team- Beşiktaş! And, according to him: the question of which team our daughter was 'born supporting' was always a no-brainer. That's right- Dalya was one of those babies with 'I love Beşiktaş' onesies.

Political affiliations and sports teams being but minor components, socialization- last but not least- became my kryptonite. My traumatic weakness which at times also had the power to catalyze me toward 'better' pastures. It often felt like long-lasting friendship cliques I observed were subconsciously based on either their members' shared periodic experiences or cultural 'sameness' in one way or another.

Friends swearing closeness 'forever' often faded out with the end of common addresses or mutual benefits and experiences. You had a car, for example? People befriended you, but often didn't reach out when they didn't need to be driven around anymore for whatever reason. I didn't drive at the time, but I did have a social mother involved heavily in Turkish-American civil society- which often aided in annual Turkish parade placements or event entrances. I had one specific Turkish-American friend, for example, whose suddenly-frequent phone calls to hang out curiously faded just as 'suddenly' when my mother's second term as the head of a particular women's civil-society group ended.

Even recently in my life as a parent, I've noticed that many mothers engage one another in conversation when their kids take classes together, only to disengage when those classes end.

Why do I mourn this rather widespread social phenomenon, you may ask, in a poetic look at biculturalism? This is the reason, dear reader; although cultural similarities didn't really seem to make a difference as a basis for friendships when such women had shared experiences- when those commonalities ended, the same women seemingly always kept their friends of similar socio-cultural backgrounds in one form or another.

Where would this leave me? I was 'Turkish' but not 'Turkic' enough to feel zeal about observing cultural holidays perfectly or greetings house guests with the sanitary *kolonya* (in retrospect, not a bad idea in our pandemic times). I was 'American' but not 'red, white and blue' enough to care much for ball games, hot dogs (still associated by many to have *haram,* pork ingredients even if they're said to be made of beef) or watching reality shows while baking apple pies.

Many fellow Turkish-Americans I was hanging out with during the aforementioned 'periods of convenience and common experiences' were experiencing similar confusions. They loved dating, but often in secret. They loved clubbing until early morning hours, but had to frequently inform their parents of their whereabouts. They loved trendy clothes, but the girls had to watch out for miniskirts or décolletage that would be deemed 'unmarriageable' by their moms' circles- often eyeing them as potential spouses for their sons or nephews. It should be no wonder the periodic friends I had tended to be either such fellow Turkish-Americans, or immigrants from other cultures who were also able to commiserate with me.

Where did we fit in? Some would say that a 'melting pot' city like New York City was the perfect place. Yet whenever I agreed, and felt 'normal' riding a subway car full of a myriad of colors and nationalities, the 'traditional voice' in my head (interestingly often sounding like the one of my mother) didn't quite feel at ease trying to avoid the strong stench of Koran-banned bacon, for example, or watching teenagers making out heavily in public.

I heard someone say once that if a child grows up with an absentee parent, they never quite feel like they 'fit in' anywhere wholly, no matter what. These verses, dear reader, that 'flow' from my soul truly feel that it was my cultural upbringing's uniqueness which also defined the uniqueness of my frequent feelings of loneliness. But, allow me to play the devil's advocate for a moment. Perhaps 'psychology' has had an influence too, as good old Sigmund Freud would have said. So, a little now about my absentee father.

A CENTERED VIEW

Him

I only have three, very vague memories of my late father. Chronologically, the first is of an avid soccer fan shooing his 4-year-old daughter away from the television screen when she'd been trying to get his attention during a game.

This image haunts me every time I find myself writing a caption for a post on social media, for example, and my little girl now tries to capture *my* attention. I don't exactly shoo her - of course- but I tell her, 'Wait, Dalya, hold on,' and as soon as I do, my guilt-ridden conscience feels as if I've shunned her from my presence. As if I've locked her in her room, screaming 'leave me alone' or something else similarly extreme.

Perhaps I'm too hard on myself at times, or even too inattentive to my daughter's requests for continuously playing her made-up games with me (my attention span tends to dip after five minutes). But that memory- my first of *him*- creeps up, and I'm hit. I try my best to make it up to her. In a way he never did- and, having passed away without making amends, will never be able to do so as her grandfather by blood.

I try to make things right.

SET FREE YOUR FLOW

In a way that my stubborn mother sometimes cannot. She loves in the best way she knows how, I suppose, and sometimes even shows affection- so rarely so that it's preciously beautiful and causes both of us bittersweet tears. But I know that 'tough love' was never a relating form I was comfortable with, and have spent my entire life searching for an affectionate one.

I try to actually learn from the past and become better, rather than continue to linger there and curse it. In this way- I'm not acting in a customary or a liberal fashion (where, I suppose, I wouldn't even really think of such conscience dilemmas). I'm observing from the middle: trying to evolve in a 'centered' way through incorporating the 'best' I can observe from two different perspectives in my life.

The second memory? After my parents divorced, my father had at first tried to 'see me' for a brief period of time when I was in kindergarten, to be fair. I remember my working mother dolling me up in fashionable clothes before leaving for work, and that my late grandmother, Emine, would take me to school.

One day sticks out in particular- because it's so often juxtaposed with another memory that I've combined them in my recollection here; the day I was so afraid to face my father when he came to visit me that the teachers had to beg me to see him at the school's lobby. He subsequently tried two more attempts to see me that I recall. One was when he bought me a bicycle and

A CENTERED VIEW

left it at the door to our house (once again I remember being afraid to greet him at the door even at least to say 'thanks'). The other was when he left a VHS tape of the then newly-released '*The Little Mermaid'* Disney movie at our neighbor's house- where I was on a playdate- and I just thanked him quietly at the door. No hug. No going off anywhere with him. I just frozen- numbed, emotionless- and I suppose at that age, only after being nudged by my teacher and neighbor who was babysitting me, respectively, thanked him to be polite.

I cried with his memory as my daughter had a mermaid-themed 5th birthday party- more because her own father calls her his 'little mermaid' in his letters, and has always coincidentally called me his 'mermaid'. Being a Turkish navy man, Kemal has always likened himself to a ship's 'captain', and hence the romanticization of the titles. I never told him about my father's memory in connection with a 'mermaid' until the prison letter I wrote to him to describe our daughter's birthday party. The prison thing is merely one of the many 'random', 'movie-like' melodramatic aspects of my life; so much so that I've come to accept discussing it on a whim. Perhaps even as catharsis, in an attempt to normalize all the craziness I've experienced.

For a week or two prior to my father's gift gestures, I'd witnessed him walking violently toward my mother during their unamicable divorce process, breaking the door to our apartment before he'd done so. I'd hid behind a couch in the living room and shut my ears and eyes. My mother later told me he'd come for some off his stuff. He hadn't said goodbye, apologized or anything to acknowledge my presence and utter shock at the entire situation as his offspring before he left.

My father had, knowingly or not, left the bicycle as his 'parting gift' at the door. I was never able to ride a bicycle since. The artist who could create amazing charcoal drawings had given me his creative genes, though not his ability to say goodbye.

A therapist I've been talking to for 'post traumatic stress disorder' (after my husband's imprisonment) has in fact shared with me how it truly does appear that my 'inability to say goodbye' to hurtful people and situations in my life stems partly from never having been able to obtain closure with the abrupt absence of my father.

But, I digress. I come now, dear reader, to my third major memory of 'him'. Walking with *the other woman*. The woman fulfilling his ambitious side, as she'd promised him a life in England. They'd end up getting married and living in England, where my half-brother Cemre was born and raised; for many years until our father's death, I'd had a half-brother without my knowledge. In the direction opposite to their walking path, my mother and I had been in the backseat of the car my late uncle Aydın was driving. We were heading to the shopping center to exchange a Mother's Day gift (a green t-shirt I never forget) I'd bought my mother in the wrong size.

My mother saw that I saw. Because she hugged me and tried to get me to turn around. My uncle tried to distract me.

But I'd seen him, and he'd seen me. And he knew he'd been seen. Right as the car had slowed down to a stop at the traffic lights, I turned around to look him in the eye from the back window. And he'd turned around- still holding her hand, despite having a sheepish look on his handsome face. We locked eyes. That was the last time I ever saw my birth father. I was five years old.

I tried contacting him as a teenager at the Turkish embassy of London, where I knew he was living with that woman. But he turned down my requests for communication.

He died of cancerous stomach/intestinal complications at the age of 50, right as I'd been turning in my final graduate thesis paper. Accordance to letters he'd written to his brother (my paternal uncle Sefer gave them to me after his death), he was 'full of regrets' and never got to achieve his big 'Western' dreams. I never got to ask him 'why did you leave ME too', and my mother never got to ask him 'how COULD you!?' She's been haunted with his betrayal for years and years- occasionally haunting *me* still, as his 'viceroy', through that brutal phrase I grew up hearing: "You're just like him".

Sometimes it was about how I looked like him or was artistic like him (the man could draw and apparently did interior design in England). But, most of the time it was whenever I'd done something 'liberal' my mother did not approve of. "You're wild and ungrateful for your family, like he was".

I was him, yes, but I was my mother too.

I still am. Both of them. Both 'east' and 'west', 'good' and 'bad' (whatever that means- I believe it's all about perspective), 'traditional' and 'liberal', 'conservative' and 'free-spirited', etc.

I grew up with dualities, dear reader. Therefore, I was torn not just between different cultures, but also between pretty much every other polarizing adjective one can think of: symbolically-characterized to me since childhood through 'my mother' versus 'my father'. I write this 'drop' out. I'm bleeding out this ink as art onto paper: this 'blood' drop, lineage portion of my centered view.

Father, I will never fully understand why you couldn't face contacting me- even in your dying days and even after you'd found me on social media as you told your brother. I could have gotten closure that may have helped me to be stronger in my mostly vulnerable relations with men during my entire life.

Mother, I will never fully understand why you could

A CENTERED VIEW

never see that I am literally half of him- yes, but also half of you- and, in unison, all together a THIRD and neutral, separate human being. Why did I have to grow up hearing about all his wrongs constantly- making me afraid of the similar characteristics in my own self? Why did I have to suffer, in a way, for *his* mistakes?

However,

Father, I forgive you.
Mother, I forgive you.
Out of respect, love, yes.
But, ultimately now in my thirties: because I forgive myself.
I forgive myself because in hindsight and reflection, I understand better why I did everything that I did. The parts of me that were at times judgmental and traditional, and at other times 'wild' and liberal;
I understand, and forgive them all.
I accept my familial, lineal trauma.
And in that acceptance and forgiveness,
I heal

Inheritance

I first read about the possibility of humans 'inheriting' lineal trauma in the James Redfield novel, *The Celestine Prophecy*- and it resonated with me immediately. I've often thought the same as many of the premises of the book: not only the part about familial-trauma inheritance, but also the concept of universal oneness. The novel- if you're unfamiliar- discusses the concept of super human capabilities for awareness and enlightenment, going through 'shifts in consciousness' and observing 'signs from the universe', such as people beginning to think and feel the same things and gradually recognizing their strengths. (Perhaps it was no 'coincidence' but rather a 'sign', then, that I thought the same).

In *Write Out Your Drops*, I bring forth the idea that our individual 'drops' or stories into the collective 'whole' of the human race (or, 'ocean') can actually resonate more with some people than we can ever fathom. The individual can be more universal than we realize. We can 'inherit' not only familial genes and traumas, but also that of those in our social circles- including people with whom we share similar cultural experiences.

In that vein, allow me to now briefly go into 'individual' drops with details that could potentially resonate with a reader who- at first glance- perhaps wouldn't even think they have much in common with myself. I've already discussed my grandparents and mother, and dedicated a subsection to my birth father. I would now like to do the same with my beloved late uncle (*dayı/m*) Aydın as well as my stepfather, 'daddy', Mert (in the following sub-section): and my 'inheritance' from the both of them.

Let's take a literal, palpable approach to inheritance- namely, a financial one. My mother was in a painful legal battle over real estate with my cousin following the untimely death of my maternal uncle from Alzheimer's (quicker so, we opine, after poor clinical care at a healthy facility my mother had to place him after he couldn't be cared for properly at home). Her brother, unfortunately, wasn't very fortuitous when it came to his personal life. (Fortunately, the judge in that case saw through his ex-wife and son's libelous self-victimization efforts, and that all they were really after was money and property)

Aydın *dayım* was always like a father-figure to me. Not just from the time after my birth one, Zafer, had left to when my mother remarried and I was lucky to get a kind-hearted stepdad, but also whenever I'd visit Turkey throughout my life. When I was working by myself in Istanbul, he was living at the time with his wife and son in a nearby home in Istanbul, and every day after work he'd make sure to ask me too whether I needed anything to be dropped off. (He drove where I didn't, so he could, for example, stock my fridge with heavy bags of fruits and vegetables that I couldn't really be expected to carry from the supermarket).

He also taught me the definition of the word 'sacrifice'. Not on the same level as my grandparents (who worked hard upon their migration to Turkey and saved enough to buy homes to leave to their two children- my mother and her brother), but on a personal-sacrifice form of attaining 'happiness' through making others happy, in order to keep a peaceful atmosphere at home. I knew that his wife and him had married young and had spent most of it fighting - the details of which I will not share here, as it is personal to them. All I know growing up was- he would meet with his sister (my mother) and I, and 'cry it out'. He would make 'Top 20' pop-music cassettes for me on my summer visits, upon my Turkish music-loving request. (He had also bought me my first 'Sony Walkman' when I was 6 years old). We'd sometimes listen to them all together on a drive, and I'd always see his eyes well up with tears at the songs.

"Don't be emotional, like your *dayı*," my mom would often warn. "Use your head over your heart. Look how his life turned out when he pitied everyone around him except himself…"

Using 'logic' in matters of the heart was accepted, like when having to say painful goodbyes to 'culturally' or 'financially' inappropriate-deemed boyfriends I'd genuinely liked. Yet my 'heart' was expected to take precedence every time I was to react 'softly' and 'respectfully' to harsh criticisms and insults for my own life's choices. Another instance where my lovely mother preached me individualism and feminist ideals, without actually accepting my choices. Her dichotomy, after all, was also full of, therefore, irony. Despite either her mind or heart undoubtedly telling her what she was preaching me, the other would always march to the beat of its own drum- anchored fixed to its own truth.

From my mother, I learned 'personal sacrifice' in terms of parenting. She, after all, left beyond socially-active jobs in Istanbul as well as her family to marry my new 'father' here in the United States- mostly for me to experience as 'normal' a family as possible

From my uncle Aydın, who too was expected to react 'softly' each time his feelings had been hurt (perhaps this was something they'd witnessed as 'the norm' from their mutual upbringing as siblings), I learned about the habitual self-sacrifice of one's pride and ego.

I can never forget his empathetic way of buying me a golden necklace and earring set during the brief time when I was living on my own in my mother's Istanbul home and paying the bills teaching English. "Your stepfather is a great man, but I want to be able to provide you with something in case of an emergency as well, since you're like a daughter to me," he'd said while giving it. My physical 'inheritance' from him. It's kept in a safe, I believe, which I haven't even peeked at for a long time. It doesn't even matter.

His real gift to me is in my memory rather than any palpable inheritance- and that's worth more than any cash I could trade in the jewelry for.

A CENTERED VIEW

Nature versus Nurture

Speaking of my mother's own dichotomous struggles and their effects on me, I would now like to talk about Mert: the Turkish-American man she remarried, whose location in New York City 'catalyzed' my coming to the United States as a little girl. Mert had come to this country himself as a child, and this is where many similarities him and I have- despite not sharing a bloodline- would begin.

He's been the sunshine to my mother's raindrops. The eternal optimist who's worked hard and long hours, with ever positive thinking and prayer, and in his 60's perhaps even 'manifested' finally owning his first beautiful home in this country.

He's been the history buff and reader to my mother's easily-bored, soap-opera lover. The scientifically-inclined engineer and HVAC specialist following magazines about space to her modern and trendy one with years in advertising and Turkish-American civil society, flipping through celebrity and fashion ones. The funny to her serious. No need to elaborate any further: he's been the yin to her yang, and I believe that this too contributed to my attempt at dichotomous harmony, aside from being reared bi-culturally.

SET FREE YOUR FLOW

Growing up, unless they were family friends who knew our histories, people who met us never even questioned whether or not he'd been my real father. He was always, God bless him, that much warm with me- but, also, we were also that much similar in personality. He too had grown up in New York with a dominant Turkish mother, and learned early on the need to laugh some things off on the outside while burying the hurt deep inside.

You know, dear reader: it occurred to me not too long ago that I've never called a man *baba*. Try to imagine a baby's classic first words. What have we often been told they could be? Most frequently they're either 'ma ma' or 'da da', in one form or another, depending on the language. In Turkish it's 'anne' and 'baba'.

I suppose as a toddler beginning to speak, I must have muttered 'baba' to my birth father on occasion, though I can't recall since I haven't seen him after age 5. I could never quite feel 'right' about calling my now dad 'baba'. Not out of coldness towards him. In fact, I would witness several American friends calling their stepparents by their names, and would think it weird and 'disrespectful' somehow. 'Baba' or even 'father/dad' always sounded too official to me. So, in my own 'centered' way as a child, I reconciled 'daddy' as being 'in the middle': somewhere between 'baba' and his name, 'Mert' or even 'Mert

A CENTERED VIEW

Abi' ('*older brother* Mert' in Turkish- a popular way of addressing people among Turks). From my 'daddy', I learned 'personal sacrifice' in regards to blood, sweat, and tear 'drops' of hard work in order to provide for your loved ones and leave behind a family legacy.

In my debut novel *The Catalyst*, I created a book trailer with a voiceover that included themes from the story. My voiceover ended with the following:

Nature, can heal
Nature, can destroy
Nature, can *catalyze*

Now, dear reader, you may or may not have read the book, but I believe it should nonetheless be clear at this point that I purposely chose this as a 'play-on-words' and used 'nature' to refer both to environmental factors like weather and plantation, but also to our *own* natures as living beings (whether human or not: hint, read *The Catalyst* to find out more). I'd like to take the opportunity to elaborate on that with this collection, and share my belief that it is not only the world around us and our own genetic inclinations which can ultimately 'catalyze' change, but the 'natures' of others too can certainly become catalysts for our various evolutions in life.

If I had never had half of my parental upbringing occur

through a Turkish-American man, for instance- who's to say I would have been able to feel the courage (and perhaps even 'freedom') to express my open-minded ideas and bold creativity?

Thank you, daddy, always, for being in my corner. Thank you, God and the Universe, for perhaps taking some things from me- yes- but providing so much more magic in return.

> *imagine your life*
> *in the way in which your soul would feel at home*
> *not only in the big moments, but even on its daily roam*
> *where you wouldn't be a second option*
> *or second-guessed*
> *but rather, for someone- the best*
> *visualize your daily tasks*
> *earning you both financial freedom*
> *as well as a spiritual kingdom*
>
> *thanking the Creator*
> *can reward every endeavor*
> *not on your hypothesized time, maybe*
> *but at the ideal time, certainly*
>
> *imagine: daily, deeply, truly*
> *accompanied then by the work and chores*
> *and, when bred by Gratitude:*
> *Poof!*
> *here it is- it's Yours!*

SECTIONAL ANECDOTES

(As a teacher, it's become habitual of me to want to do regular reviews of 'takeaways' at the ends of sections and sometimes even include 'interesting facts' or observations related to each section)

Growing up bicultural has meant...

- *feeling dichotomized between a culture dominated by 'instant wealth through inheritance' dependance and the community's prioritization over the individual in one culture, and individuality alongside of success through hard work in the other*

- *most relatives and friends 'back in the homeland' assuming you are somehow 'wealthier' than them, as you are physically living in what they deem a 'brand' name- the United States of America. Even if they're property-owners while you're renting and taking out credit/loans.*

- *being the envy of your circle during summer vacation visits, who often 'order' various brand names for you to bring for them on your flight. 'You must have so many Abercrombie jeans you can afford there', they'd say, while I'd never even heard of the brand name growing up in NYC- the dorky me who was happy with whatever brand looked nice and felt comfortable during my minimal shopping trips.*

THE SOUL'S REQUEST

her soul is akin to these woods
not as frequented
and hence often misunderstood

her eyes are gazed upon,
smile lingers in their memory
causing them to return from the vortex
of their 'freedom'
eventually

her hands are often cold
despite warmth from fingers or a glove,
with the spirit's satisfaction often disregarded
they're not the only ones that mistake convenience
for 'love'

she haunts like the woods,
yet is haunted herself by the cry of her own soul
pleading to be loved for its candor,
no other delights have made it feel whole

A CENTERED VIEW

THE MAGNET IN THE WIND

she parts her lips
to swallow air
and fills her lungs
with the current's beauty
to ease inner despair

she then throws back her hair

her flow is attached to the wind
a magnetic force clings them in unison
following one's own path isn't treason

she's attached only to the unattached
the magnet repels and attracts

like ancient artifacts
she detaches when they've latched
feigned devotion only distracts

her naïveté long ago-snatched

affections have departed
more bitter than broken-hearted

they'll deny her lasting breeze
only if they dare

she's left her mark
she was there

SET FREE YOUR FLOW

SECTION II:
Flowing Through Relationships

IMPERFECT EMPATH

A CENTERED VIEW

NAPOLEON

being the object of your
affection
was torture
both mental and moral

I cried my biographical pain
out onto you
as a notepad of comfort
yet could never quite avoid a
quarrel

by my tears, you weren't
affected
thought you deserved
obedience
from a sought gem
you made to feel rejected

*each time it refused to be what you
greedily expected*

I empathized with your
struggle
whilst you could not even
sympathize with mine

you talked the talk of an
emperor
yet walked the walk of a bear
without a spine

you sacrificed and let me be
since you couldn't set your ugly
truths free

if one cannot value the jewel
they don't deserve showing it
off as jewelry

for the one without chivalry

SET FREE YOUR FLOW

THE CAPTIVATING CAPTIVE

removed from the bustle
of busy city sidewalks,
perched on a bench stone,
the captive now inhales maneuver
and freshly-cut grass after the rain
rather than the stench of gasoline

the ears have seagulls for company
rather than police sirens
or drivers speeding by with words obscene

the seldom nature walk has now become daily routine
the busyness of the captive's mind
has become less actual business
and simpler in pleasure,
more serene

regardless,
the pearl still isn't free to roam outside its shell
a captivating captive can get captivated, yes,
while remaining captured
as well

A CENTERED VIEW

My Assumption About Assumptions

Okay. I know what you're thinking. "This is the 'relationships' portion of her writing, and she's just described her troubled/non-existent relationship with her absentee father before his death. So, she's going to now talk about all the romantic heartbreak she lived through and blame it on her childhood…" Am I right? Or did I just assume again? Yeah, I've been told I do tend to assume too quickly sometimes. It's one of my bad habits. But I honestly feel I do that at times as a preemptive defense mechanism, I suppose.

Maybe I've grown so accustomed to people assuming things about me- mostly wrongfully so- by just looking at me, that I've unintentionally nurtured that same habit as well. Furthermore, I can also at times literally and 'empathetically' sense someone's energy by how they react to something I share with them.

In this case, dear reader, I'm writing these words before you naturally get to read them- and I am no 'Baba Venga' (the late, blind psychic lady from Bulgaria: the same land of pretty much both my sets of grandparents).

But, regardless of what you may or may not have thought, don't worry (or perhaps even- sorry to disappoint): this will not, and cannot, be a romantic 'tell-all'.

True to my main purpose for writing this poetic essay collection: I will genuinely touch on all the bi-cultural dilemmas I've lived through from the perspective of dating, relationships, and even marriage, and allow them to 'flow' through me cathartically. And, yes, one such dilemma is of course precisely the reason *why* I *can't* publish some tell-all book. For if I do so, it could be deemed 'dishonorable', if I'm not ruffling some feathers already just by all that I've written thus far. (Also, of course, I'm no famous celebrity or anyone of that sort to truly gather such intrigue in my personal life anyway, so I'm purposely limiting my biographical musings only to the most relevant ones for my artistic point as a writer in this collection).

I'm no love expert, and in no way do I attempt to be. But from my experiences, dear reader, I've come to believe that in order for a relationship to best maintain harmony, there needs to be a voluntary acceptance of dual roles in a particular dynamic. In other words, there must be an acceptance of one partner's dominance and need for control as well as of the other's passivity and relaxed attitude.

From the perspective of our main theme of dual backgrounds explored, I believe that a dynamic of duality can best prolong a relationship in the most functional way. If a man and woman are both comfortable- outwardly and inwardly- with

A CENTERED VIEW

the 'traditional' role of the male as the breadwinner and the female as the homemaker, another couple where the roles are reversed should also be both respected and accepted. An entire Asian-rooted belief system, after all, similarly has praised the 'yin/yang' concept of the harmony between opposites for years, and it is not my place to go into that. The book I-Ching (I own the one translated from Chinese by Richard Wilhelm and Cary F. Baynes) describes the ridgepole (line), for instance, to describe *"...oneness' (where) duality comes into the world, for the line at the same time posits an above and a below, a right and left, front and back- in a word, the world of the opposites..."*

I can simply tell my story and share my experiences vis à vis a dualistic view situated right on that 'center' ridgepole/line.

In a lot of cultures, for example (not just Turkish, of course)- a man (whether or not he is outwardly seen as the 'masculine' and the 'breadwinner') would likely be ridiculed for showing 'obedience' to his wife and her stereotypically 'controlling' ways, especially around the house.

Let me go into another mini-sketch. (I dabbled in some theater as a student, so kindly bear with me here)

Wife: Take off those shoes closer by the door! You're bringing outside germs too far inside the house.
Husband: Yes, dear. What's for dinner?

Wife: Whatever you find left over from yesterday in the fridge. I've been busy all day. If you don't like it, you can order some takeout.

Husband: Leftovers are fine dear. Here are those plum tomatoes you asked for.

Yeah, I know what you must be thinking. "She should have been a playwright. This is some astounding dialogue (insert laughter here)". Did I also mention I love employing *sarcasm* in my daily life? Interestingly, many Turks I've met don't really use or grasp sarcasm, so I feel this is the 'American' side of me.

In any random comedy show in Turkey, the dialogue I just conjured up would typically be accompanied by some machine-laughs. Culturally, it would be considered 'funny' for a man to be so 'passive' as to do what his wife asks without questioning her or 'putting her in her place'.

Yes. What I've just said is harsh. But unfortunately, this is the sad reality of the expectations amongst many in machoistic societies. The idea that maybe, just maybe, a husband figure may actually be satisfied in such a dynamic (based on harmonious duality with his wife) is as foreign as the crater of the moon for many people. Perhaps such a man could have been raised by a domineering mother himself or have had dating experiences throughout his life that may have triggered a subconscious need

A CENTERED VIEW

for his partner to be in control of daily routines. We simply do not know.

Maybe it is none of the above. Maybe such a man simply feels comfortable giving his life partner the reins in general: where doing so doesn't make him feel weakened, but rather empowered by the relative relaxation of having to make less of the decisions himself. It's no one's business but their own what works for them- any couple in a healthy, functional relationship.

We should never assume we know what goes on behind closed doors for anyone- and yes, in my plea for people to never do this to me, I also tell this to myself. Assuming is as part of human nature, unfortunately, as jealousy or rivalry. Yet assumptions were a major component of what I've experienced as a Turkish-American growing up in New York City, and vacationing during the summertime in Turkey.

Here in the US, some assumed, for instance, that my slight accent was a result of being educated in Turkey (I never went to school in Turkey beyond 2nd grade, but spoke Turkish frequently at home due to my mother's insistence). There, in Turkey, meanwhile, they assumed I spoke English at every opportunity due to arrogance: not realizing for me it was a matter simply of comfort and natural expression.

Here, they assumed I wasn't a particularly affectionate person because outwardly I couldn't express myself as freely as my American friends could- in fear of societal judgement and familial chastisement. There, they assumed I must have 'done wild drugs at wild orgies' since I lived on campus in college (the answer is a resounding 'no' to both).

Back to my personal 'centered view'. I know some people who may be reading this can relate to my musings, even having had experienced just one dominant culture growing up. I have friends in Istanbul, for example, who say they also feel 'too Western' in their ways of thinking compared to their more traditional families- despite never having set foot outside of the country.

Regardless, from personal experience, I would still say that more Turkish-Americans struggle with this in comparison. I would even go so far as to claim that there is most certainly a Turkishness-based disease of constantly worrying about what others think rather than prioritizing individual happiness: particularly when living outside of Turkey. Was it because many of us were struggling to 'fit in' here in Western society, while simultaneously grappling to be accepted by our own social circles? Was this parallel struggle somehow making it easier for us to judge and categorize one another abroad, since our decisions were doubled in difficulty due to the additional realm in which we felt

A CENTERED VIEW

the pressure to conform?

I've seen men peer-pressured, for instance, to 'cheat on their wives' just because, as the man, they 'could' and 'should'. I've also seen women peer-pressured to 'accept' a cheating (or even violent) spouse: as long as they had a roof over their head and could maintain the social illusion of being in a 'happy marriage'! It was just 'dirt on a man's hand' (*elinin kiri*), as the Turkish expression goes, that the man could just 'wash off'. I've even met a young man who had to lie to his mother that his boyfriend was a woman, and who later had to get married to reproduce children- where he had to lead his 'secret life' as a gay man behind closed doors.

Turkey- my homeland of many ironies- tends to condemn homosexuality as a 'disease' that can be solved by religion, while publicly celebrating many transgender singers and celebrities over many decades.

As a child vacationing in Turkey, I would see more transgender prostitutes than women waiting on street corners at night- even in traditionally conservative neighborhoods. Sexual identity is merely one example of irony in Turkey; I will not even go into how covered and uncovered women have been made to stand against one another for decades by men, or how pedophiles have been excused by clergy misusing religious text in different contexts to normalize their crimes.

SET FREE YOUR FLOW

How the globally-renowned, Turkish-origin founders of the Pfizer/BioNTech coronavirus vaccine in Germany have not been as celebrated by many Turks due to their 'Alevi' faith (a different sect of Islam than the popular Sunni one of Turkey). Or even how the talented Elif Shafak- a world-famous Turkish writer (who writes in English as well) suddenly stopped being pointed out as a role model for my writing amongst some in my circle the moment she recently came out as bisexual.

(Yes. There. I 'went into it'. I know. But I've kept it as brief as I can. It was simply unavoidable).

I've seen parents advocate 'bad in private/ good on paper' dates to their children as potential spouses- not just out of potential financial desperation, but also a social one. And I've heard first-hand of girls engaging in Islamically-taboo anal sex: not by choice, but in order to avoid the even bigger 'taboo' of not being discovered to be 'virgins' on their wedding nights.

Speaking of sex. Let's flow right into our next section.

A CENTERED VIEW

Darn You Arianna Grande and Bruno Mars

"So what you doin' tonight?" "I'm gonna leave the door open...tell me that you're coming through..."

Lyrics like these from so many artists frequently played on the radio, are NOT lyrics that this bi-cultural girl has ever able to listen to lightly. We can love them and their songs as artists (love you Arianna and Bruno), but nonetheless feel immense frustration every time their lyrics indirectly remind us of our internal struggles.

When you've got Turkish parents, even if you're 18, there's no way any significant other is going to be able to casually 'come over' to your place (if you're actually living on your own at that point as Turkish-American youth, you're a rarity). Nor can you ever go over to theirs, unless you've created about 3 separate scenarios (in case one falls through) that you can lie about and which mostly involve hanging out with your girlfriends in one way or another.

Now, in no way do I condone lying to parents. Especially my younger readers; as much as it may hurt sometimes to potentially be yelled at, risking meeting a stranger somewhere unsafe is never a good idea, so at the very least always make sure SOMEONE you trust knows where you really are at all times.

So why then, if I don't advocate lying, am I writing about it? Because no Turkish-American friend I've met has ever NOT had to do it, due to at times unrealistic and grandiose parental expectations of absolute *holy* behavior from their children.

Whether myself or my friends 'lost' our 'virginities' before marriage or not isn't the issue here, nor is it anyone's business, so I will now diplomatically step aside from addressing that. Rather, my point is as follows.

The concept of even 'casually' hanging out with anyone of the opposite gender was always so 'grand' for our parents that they only really saw doing so as 'black and white': either to potentially spend time to 'get to know' someone 'marriage material' on a 'serious, clean date', OR, to spend platonic time in a GROUP setting (preferably with friends familiar to them there with us as well).

Let's now cue a Tik Tok-like, exemplary sketch.

A.
The Parent: "Where have you been!?"

Their child: "Oh you know, with (insert familiar friend's name

A CENTERED VIEW

here) **at** (insert 'safe' location here)**"**

The Parent: "Hmm, was there anyone else with you all?"

Their child: "Oh, just some other friends they know. (Immediately add an attempt to switch the conversation) **The food/view was great! Oh my God, we have to go there as a family sometime…"**

The Parent: "Hmm…I see. Was there anyone interesting in particular?"

OR,

B. *(after a bad date with someone your parents tried to set you up with)*
The Parent: "How was dinner, honey?"

The Child: "Oh, it was okay. I'm going up to my room. I still have some work…"

The Parent: "What did you guys eat? What did you talk about? Did you find out his/her car/job/parents' job (insert whatever status icon you can think of here)**?**

The Child: "Not really. It wasn't anything special. We'll talk later…You know, you never asked these questions last week

when I had a great time with my friend… (insert name of someone you actually like that they don't approve of)."

In parental defense, especially as I am one now: I am more and more aware with each passing day that this is – in a parent's mind at least- ultimately to 'help' us 'be happy in the long run' with someone deemed 'suitable' for us. The sad reality, however, is that there's never any 'magic formula', in my experience, when it comes to matters of the heart.

I've witnessed dates between two people 'good' for each other 'on paper' that never went anywhere- despite physical attractiveness. I've witnessed dates between people that went quite well-much to many people's surprise, since at first glance no one would have paired the two of them together for whatever 'logical' reasoning (mainly involving credentials).

However, to be fair, I've also seen dating situations where a child didn't heed to his or her parents' warnings about someone, and it turned out that the parent was right- that person really turned out to be a heartbreaker.

So, what is any bicultural child to do? One walking on eggshells to both exert his/her 'individual' choice to follow his/her 'dreams' in a way continuously advocated by Western culture AND simultaneously 'honor' their family and traditions as well?

A girl in love with someone she 'shouldn't' be? A boy

who wants to go into the music industry rather than take over his father's architectural business? What's the best course of action for such youth?

I wish I could insert here some pearl of wisdom that I've finally learned after all my trials and tribulations. And, certainly, Lord knows there are enough such self-help works out there published by people who I'm sure have done research on the issue much lengthier than I ever could.

But, alas, my only formula would be, in all honesty: trial and error, vis-à-vis *surrendering to the flow of life*.

That's right.

Aside from the implication of finding your own unique cultural-combination path in life, my implication for the title of this poetic collection itself is to surrender to the 'catalyst' winds directing you towards the most ideal path for you. These currents tend to flow from your inner voice when you meditate or pray in quiet, your instincts, repeated experiences which cannot be coincidences but rather celestial attempts to teach you a lesson, and- finally- universal signs.

Let's consider my 'mate selection', as an example, alongside my 'surrendering' to certain 'signs' that I noticed in my life. The same father who'd left both my mother and myself

SET FREE YOUR FLOW

in my native Istanbul to form another family abroad, was of the astrological sign of Scorpio. Heeding to my mother's warnings throughout my dating years, I never even ended up dating any Scorpio- until I married one at age 27! My mother was no astrological expert, but I grew up continuously being warned to 'stay away' from Scorpio men. As fellow Leo women, they weren't 'compatible' with us, she said, and the union would only 'result in disaster'.

Life is said to be what happens when you're busy making other plans, however, and it turned out that Kemal, my daughter's currently innocently-imprisoned father, is not only a Scorpio- but also happens to have a birthday that falls one day before my late father's (albeit in a different year, of course). Here's another, seemingly smaller one: my father was also, I've been told, an avid *Beşiktaş* fan, and I never dated one until- you guessed it- I married Kemal in all his Beşiktaş-admiring glory.

My mother was so traumatized by having 'given her all' to her first 'major love' as a young adult (they'd both gotten married at age 21, and from my current view as an adult, it seems to me they were both practically kids) and then subsequently having been betrayed, that she repeatedly warned me of men similar to my father in any way or fashion- most prominently, their astrological sign.

Ironically, however, she would also tell me stories of

how 'blissfully happy' the two of them had been- until he'd met 'that other woman' at his work place. It's also interesting to me that my Scorpio father ended up marrying a Pisces woman, whereas my Scorpio husband Kemal's first wife- from whom he'd gotten divorced when we were introduced- was also a Pisces. That's one Scorpio-Pisces couple that stood the test of time and another that didn't (so much for astrological signs as reliable predictors of marriage compatibility).

"This is the way things are in life…."

It's what many of us often heard growing up. "It's our job to be realistic for your own good". This always seemed to me to be a core component of Turkish culture- especially among families trying to 'keep it alive' abroad, like mine.

Family rules were never supposed to make sense, I realize now in retrospect. Just respected. And unquestioned. "Why?" we'd ask. "Because we are the parents. We have the experience. Respecting your parents is in the Koran, as well. No one wants the best for you except your parents". That's what I- and many friends in similar bi-cultural households- grew up hearing.

Chastisement of offspring- particularly daughters, in fact- is such an inherent part of Turkish culture that there's a proverb that roughly translates to, "…those who do not discipline their daughters are doomed to beat their own selves up…" I won't even go into the obvious controversial nature of this seemingly violence-supporting proverb, dear reader, as it is not my point here. What I've always had the most trouble with has been the *double standards* placed on young Turkish girls- especially those raised abroad like myself or at least in 'western/secular' parts of Turkish society despite more traditional familial backgrounds.

Had I subconsciously married a Scorpio to 'spite' my mother? I doubt it. I'd dated far more controversial and 'out there' guys before my husband, after all, whom she didn't approve of for reasons beyond relatively more innocent qualities such as their 'incompatible' birthdays. No. In fact, when I was first introduced to my husband by our relatives attempting 'matchmaking'- I'd always thought we'd just be friends, and I kept my distance romantically for a good two years or so. (Frankly, I'd found the military lifestyle- unfamiliar to my upbringing- rather 'boring')

That is exactly why I believe that, in a way, it was also 'fate' that I would end up attracting something to myself I'd most 'thought about' to actually please my mother: 'Avoid Scorpio men at all costs'.

Perhaps we end up living out what we most try to avoid. Perhaps the reason we even end up trying to avoid that 'thing', in fact, is it could possibly even be a

A CENTERED VIEW

part of our soul's flow- and our focus on it has always been a 'sign' from the universe after all, one which we must eventually face.

Come to think of it, I see now through living with my mother back in New York (while Kemal remains politically-imprisoned), in fact, that my mother has a lot in common with him! Could Sigmund Freud have been right? Do we all subconsciously 'flow' and gravitate toward people who remind us of the familiarity of our childhoods- whether or not that familiarity is a warm or toxic one? We can never know all the answers for certain. I'll leave that philosophical question be for now, and continue with my next sub-section.

So, speaking of double standards, let's turn the page to explore it further, ladies and gents.

SET FREE YOUR FLOW

Women as 'Prey' and Men as the 'Predators'

Hey, let's go on a weekend getaway to somewhere near the water (summer time), or, some cabin to ski (winter time)…

And CUT. The Hollywood-fantasy daydream would certainly end there for many Turkish-American youth- especially girls. For, of course, 'staying the night' anywhere but in a home environment 'protected' by elders implies the possibility at least of some 'men' sniffing women out as 'prey'. The possibility of luring us into their hotel rooms, or finding some way to manage themselves into ours.

This is but one scenario out of many, of course. And, yes, I'm aware that- as with every cultural group- exceptions exist. Had I heard of Turkish-American girls being able to go on weekend getaways with a mixed-gender group of friends? Absolutely, although these exceptions too were almost always able to exist precisely on the condition that the exact list of people who'd be with them was made known (preferably youth whose families the parents knew and trusted). Frequent phone check-ins were also conducted, with photographed proof that the traveler hadn't actually ventured off with some lover somewhere.

Now, I have to insert here- in fairness to my parents- that I was, on a couple of occasions, able to travel and spend the night without them somewhere (having fulfilled the unspoken-contractual 'conditions' I've outlined above).

However, and this is why I even mention this example in this portion of the book: there was one eventful incident where I spent one evening in another US city while traveling with a female friend (hence, my parents had allowed it). We'd had an unspoken male friend accompanying us: a known diplomat representing Turkey at the United Nations at the time. He was single and friendly, and, despite his older age: we'd trusted him. In our naïveté – we'd viewed him as an 'older brother figure'. Did he proceed to hit on me that evening and make me uncomfortable throughout our journey? You bet your bottom dollar he did.

Okay, dear reader, I promised I wouldn't give 'the juice' too much, since I do not intend for my poetic and cultural essay collection to turn into some 'tell-all', if you recall, so I will cut that part of my story there. His identity isn't relevant here. But what I ponder often- as well as what I feel becomes especially difficult growing up bicultural- is the following. In hindsight, I can now, in my 30's, reflect back on my experiences and wonder what the 'other' sides must have thought- with many having been conditioned with the 'machoism' of Turkish culture. Now, in no way do I wish to generalize about Turkish men or insult anyone except the outlying exceptions I've experienced (who should indeed be ashamed of themselves if they ever come across these words).

Like the well-known politician in Turkey also, for example, who lifted my skirt and massaged my shoulders suggestively when I'd visited his office as a family friend, trusting him to give me- as a recent political scientist graduate- professional advice.

I'd gone to him to check out my CV, rather than my legs. He undoubtedly searched for any 'welcoming' hints from me that would have otherwise possibly caused him to go further- which also suggested to me that this was likely not his first attempt to cross the line, nor would it be his last. What did I do? I froze. And I vaguely recall afterward pretending it didn't happen, wiggling away from his touch and taking my CV in my hand to change the topic, both in shock and denial in that moment.

So, technically- no, I was never violated by any Turkish man. I was, however, forcibly kissed despite saying 'no' and 'stop' to two *non-Turkish* men while I was living on campus in college in Long Island. Even younger- when I was a junior high school student riding the Queens city bus to my school- I was harassed by a straphanger man of a different ethnicity. He'd sneered suggestively as he inched his organ close to my frozen-in-fear face until I'd run out of the bus one stop early in tears: running to school so that he wouldn't follow me.

Indeed, a harassing-temperament doesn't discriminate based on background. What goes through the mind of any sexual predator is a topic too huge for me to explore. So, rather, the culturally-relevant and specific dilemma I presently intend to explore is this: *what had made the Turkish men in particular- with their positions of power- feel they could do what they did, and get away with it?* I opine that, assured silence- unfortunately and undoubtedly- would likely come at the top of the list, right before their sense of 'entitlement'. They knew that I wouldn't say anything to my parents- who knew them- because I'd feel embarrassed in our mutual social circles. They knew my mother especially wanted them to help me, as 'older brother figures', to 'land a good job'.

That possibility of 'a good job' with their 'connections' was always dangled in front of me like a toy to a cat. A promise that never materialized. A promise they treated like a bribe- as if I was somehow expected to render some 'service' in exchange for a 'good job' in their circle- despite my qualifications sincerely fulfilling the requirements of such positions in the first place.

Dear reader…You can imagine, as someone especially with these experiences, that I've rejoiced the recent empowerment of the Me-Too movement. I always aim to have 'a view from the middle', however, and gender happens to be one of them. I always try to be fair. Just as I've mentioned agreeing with 'the other' political party on certain issues, there were one or two testimonies from a couple of publicized statements where it honestly felt to me like the man being accused was more of a victim than the woman.

Regardless, those instances were few and far in between. Many of those women displayed tremendous courage to be able to speak out, and I am so proud of the moment overall. I was seldom one to ask, 'why did they wait so long?' For I know, from firsthand experience, that sometimes you just can't speak out. For me, the reason included my aforementioned cultural reasons: fear of professional setbacks, bringing shame- or worse- threats to my family's name, embarrassment, etc.

Perhaps those women had tried to move on from their experiences, until hearing about other women's accusations 'catalyzed' them to finally feel empowered enough to speak out later on through the support of numbers. In my case, for example, I know for sure I'm not the only young woman that

A CENTERED VIEW

particular man hit on in Turkey. In fact, I had a good platonic guy friend in Turkey for many years from the politician's very circle who warned me against both him as well as a couple of his other known colleagues in Ankara (the country's capital). "Don't go on that job interview there," he'd warn. "We all know about (his) come-ons to young women. You're a good person. I don't want you to go through that".

Needless to say- especially after my skirt-lifting experience at this point- I heeded my friend's advice, and never went on that particular interview. What would have happened if I had? The AK Party in power in Turkey had seriously wanted me to get involved with them politically, I can tell you that much. Most recently before my relocation to Norway as a married woman in 2012 (in 2011, in fact) they'd offered me to join their 'Youth' organization in the secularized and trendy 'Kadıköy' district of Istanbul where I'd been living. They said they could 'use' more women without headscarves on their team to show their 'inclusivity'.

Would I have been able to spare myself from the affections of that politician with the 'roving-eye' in Ankara had I met him? Would I have been able to genuinely obtain an influential-enough post within the political party to somehow now been able to get my innocently-imprisoned husband out of prison? Or, would they have faultily accused me of being a member of their contemporary choice as 'the other' in Turkey: FETO- and have sacked me (or, worse, imprisoned) before I could do so? (FETO is the name given to alleged members of the Gülenist movement the Erdoğan government accuses of having plotted a coup attempt in order to topple him).

I will never know.

I did, in fact, contact that platonic friend in AK party to relay my husband's genuine innocence and asked if they could help him. "There are so many like him. We can't help them either. Sorry. We are afraid, too, and are powerless in this situation..." was his response.

What can I say? I can only continue to pray and advocate on behalf of justice for the innocently-accused since 2016: sharing my truths, as everyone who knows me and my family can testify that I am not, never will be nor have ever been associated with Gülen in any shape or form, and neither has my husband. If he had been, I could never had gotten married to someone with such different ideologies from mine.

I do not wish to digress further into politics, so I will now return to my main theme for this subheading, dear reader. *Women as 'prey', men as 'predators'.* There are so many subcomponents to this that it's difficult to choose just one to narrow in on for the purpose of my poetic essay collection here.

Shall I explore that curious acceptance of many

A CENTERED VIEW

transgendered people as singers and celebrities in Turkey for decades- while casting stones (only proverbial ones, as Turkey is still luckily secular country as I write this collection) on gay couples (no publicly 'out' couples can be seen in the Turkish media)? Or perhaps go into the sad dogma still followed by many traditional mindsets that women are 'secondary' to men in 'worth' and should therefore be acceptant of being 'disciplined' physically or cheated on by their husbands? How various forms of abuse tend not to be interfered in- due to them being an *aile meselesi* (a 'family issue') that authorities do not want to get involved in?

What about the cultural disregard for a woman actually desiring someone and going after them- despite sexuality being natural for both genders, and a premarital sin being a 'sin' (according to the Koran) for both women *and* men? I've literally heard Turkish-American parents warn their daughters against men as the 'big bad wolves' that could entice them in bars or clubs for physical intimacy. They'd be told to 'guard' themselves- as the 'sheep'- against the 'barbaric desires of men': ignoring that attraction and desire could at times be consensual and mutual. Such warnings occur in Turkey as well- of course- yet abroad, there tends to be a larger assumption that non-Turkish men will somehow not 'respect' our 'virtue' as much. Personally, I feel that if someone is a predator, they're a predator everywhere. They'll just use different tactics, i.e. false promises of love in one and further false promises of marriage in another.

I won't, dear reader. For these are universal issues that perhaps I'm only partial to exploring due to the intensity of femicides being covered on Turkish news; so much so that a black and white image-sharing of international women in support occurred during the summer of 2020 on social media. Though it occurs everywhere and certainly so here in the United States as well: in Turkey, femicide feels comparatively grander in scale, due to the geographically smaller size of the nation.

I will further explore, instead, that I was targeted and 'coincidentally' approached by the 'Adnan Oktar' cult in Istanbul. For decades, they were known to brainwash young educated people (especially women they found to be attractive and later attempted to fit into a certain voluptuous-look through plastic surgery) with promises of 'good jobs' and an affluent lifestyle. Many of its members have recently been imprisoned, and, especially due to my sensitivity for imprisonment in general, I will not say anything about that here. All I will say is that I was spared and lucky to have been able to 'get out' before I was ever 'initiated' by the grace of God. But anyone curious about that brief chapter of my life has to look no further than the way I've symbolically and indirectly portrayed them in my novel, *'The Catalyst'* (as well as in its sequel, *'The Penance'*).

A CENTERED VIEW

That's all I will say about them.

So why mention them at all? Surely cults- especially those luring young women to carry out their perverse fantasies and 'missions'- have been around for centuries and in many cultures around the world (including ones with celebrities, as seen recently on the news right here in the United States). However, once again, vis-à-vis Turkish culture in general: I have to think of what this means on a broader, sociological scale.

Allow me to assume once again, dear reader, before I go any further. Perhaps you are now asking- *okay, but, umm, Selin, wasn't this meant to be an exploration of setting free your true self despite the difficulties of growing up as a bicultural person, and not a sole study of Turkish culture in general?*

Absolutely.

I mention the Oktar cult specifically for this reason; they aimed to mostly target women who spoke English, to be used as 'honey traps' (espionage using attractive promises of relations) to lure affluent businessmen and politicians and obtain government information. One of their many controversial components was the sexualized-look of their 'disciples' on Oktar's television channel. A look of décolletage and miniskirts (often showing these women dancing seductively around him like some stereotypical Sultan) that contrasted directly with the principle of *modesty* in Islam. They claimed to want to 'ameliorate' the 'bad reputation' of Islam in the world, referring to many still unfortunately linking the peaceful religion with terrorism and extremism in many ways.

Their religion-based discussions were extremely 'Eastern' while their look was extremely of the 'West'. I would love to eventually hear interviews with some of the young women in that cult to find out how-on the inside- they dealt with being dichotomous in such an ostentatious way on the outside.

Finally, I will conclude this section by saying the following. In no way do I mean to express any antagonist views against people (Turkish, American, Turkish-American, or of any cultural category) who genuinely for themselves and religious reasons wish to be/marry an 'honorable bride' (or groom! You have to be fair!). Rather, I express sadness at the lack of ease in obtaining such an ideal in our modern society. My commentary isn't merely about virginity or lack thereof. It is merely about the pure difficulty of finding someone you can spiritually, emotionally, mentally and physically feel connected with in our day and age without being faced with various *double standards* and *hypocritical customs*.

Things are rough enough as they are with the additional temptations of social media which did not *exist during the time of our 'forefathers' and grandmothers.*

If a young man and woman can still marry today- either for love, or for familial support/ respect that can grow into love- and grow old together…that's amazing! I would love it if such rare couples of our modern era could share more of their stories to give all of us hope! But let's try to take an honest look all around us. All we hear about are romantic failures- either due to various infidelities or economic/socio-cultural woes.

How can a woman be expected to have restrained from any form of physical affection with the opposite gender up until age 25- the average age when modern girls are encouraged to get married in our circles, after having obtained higher education and 'some job experience for social standing' (and, of course, for meeting eligible men)?

How can a man be expected to have- on his own (not just borrowing heavily from his father's pockets or 'inheriting' professional influence)- be able to have accumulated enough status and money to be deemed ready for marriage?

What ends up happening, then? Very often I've heard around me of a young man and woman falling in love, for example, and having to date secretly from the girl's parents. Only to eventually (and heartbreakingly) break up because they would realize their feelings getting deeper as time (and youthful opportunities) would be 'fleeting' by. 'Why', they'd ask themselves, should they 'continue the relationship if the possibility for a socially-acceptable marriage doesn't exist' for them?

Very often, social/regional discrepancies are used as excuses for young couples not to get married among Turks ("You can't marry him- his family consists of villagers from the East!" or "You can't marry her- she's not from the Black Sea region like us!"). The twosome, then, realize their families will never support them- and, often needing their support mostly financially- they end up parting ways in tears, listening to popular Turkish 'blues' music called 'Arabesk' and other similarly sad songs.

They tend to watch the gazillions of globally-trendy Turkish soap operas- *diziler*- which then capitalize on such storylines, and air nightly/weekly for three hours (longer than most Hollywood movies) to distract the public from the tragedy of domestic news. Yet, of course, this social unacceptance very often does not mean their love wasn't real- so, very often, by this point they'll have had gotten intimate with one another, as God created our natures to express. Ideally- in a marriage- sure.

Dear reader. I'm a firm believer that the Koran was meant to strengthen out faiths and 'guide us' with maxims for 'optimal happiness' in our lives over the long-run- not as some

A CENTERED VIEW

set of rigid rules deserving 'punishment' upon the slightest disobedience. But what if society- for the various economic and socio-cultural reasons mentioned- doesn't allow for such a marriage to be supported? Hence, the aforementioned scenario is merely one out of many in which couples end up being intimate- often for the right reasons of love, too- and yet cannot get married due mostly to familial interference.

Sexuality. The ever taboo. Especially for dichotomously-torn Turks. The unmentioned, yet certainly noticed, proverbial elephant in any Turkish-American room. As human beings, it is an inherent and undeniable force within all of us- with its seeds and urges budding since childhood- and simply has to be addressed. Perhaps it'll be befitting, dear reader, to end this section- which I started with song lyrics- with a reference to another set of popular lyrics. Namely, the one of 'Let It Go' from the Disney animated feature, 'Frozen'.

"Be the good girl you always have to be…conceal, don't feel …. don't let them know… well, now they know…let the storm rage on…" Thank you, Elsa (of, 'coincidentally', beautiful Norway that catalyzed me to write 'The Catalyst'). I'm allowing my inner 'flow' to 'blow' strongly enough to create a literary 'current', and counteract any culturally-expectant and 'raging storm' they can hurl toward me.

SECTIONAL ANECDOTES

Growing up bicultural has meant:

- having to keep quiet about influential family acquaintances- such as an older 'family man' and politician you'd trusted for professional advice and internship opportunities, only to have him 'test the waters' with you through a lifting of your skirt and an invasion of your personal space with an unsolicited neck massage

- feigning that you're not interested in anyone outside of someone good on paper/on a path to marriage: because- as a woman- why would you have interest in anything other than becoming an 'honorable' and 'beautiful' bride, on a path to eventually become a mother? *It is,* they'd claim, after all, *the men with the animalistic need*: where the sex they desire and have can be 'washed off' like 'dirt off a hand', while the same 'dirt' would haunt a girl's reputation. That's why all those precious/ over-exaggerated golden jewels are placed on a bride (she must be the 'virgin prize'), alongside of a red ribbon around the waist of her wedding gown to symbolize the virginal 'blood' traditionally required to be 'spilled' that night.

- being told, growing up, to not let men 'use and discard you like a napkin'- even when the closeness may have been consensual. Where you cannot admit- sometimes even to yourself (unless you're 'a bad woman')- that those feelings were indeed mutual.

A CENTERED VIEW

OUCH

the narcissist wonders why the
empath has finally
had enough
and in typical fashion,
quite possibly
even suspects the empath of
having allowed for another's
seduction

yes, the empath has finally
severed ties
cutting them off with a
proverbial blade
though never sharper than the
always brutal, painful cut of the
narcissist's cyclical words

only this time, not on purpose
through the way of tears
or some forced 'silent
treatment' game

the cut has simply developed
naturally
indifference and neutrality:
reaction from a soul weary
of having been mistreated for
so long

the empath has been rescued
by another love, indeed
the unmistakable,
incomparable and whole love
she's found
within her whole self

and by doing so- she's being
loved by the universe in return

the narcissist cannot compete
and has thus become obsolete

SET FREE YOUR FLOW

BIRDS

the fumbling chick, awkward still in flight
flutters before us, naïve to the potential danger
of a malevolent human's might

unlike its momma sparrow- who is, nonetheless,
risking her life to ensure her offspring can survive another day
for her to feed, nest and caress

one's adventure and experience
is the other's protective bravery
we're oblivious to which role we ourselves fulfill
fluttering about until intervened by destiny

we linger
like nestlings
with inadequate wings

A CENTERED VIEW

SECTION III: Flowing Through Socialization

EXTRAVERTED INTROVERT

SET FREE YOUR FLOW

EYES IN BLOOM

is it the birds chirping
that sets my heart audibly beating?
and my heart blooming?
or, is it the revival of hope and life
that the pending spring tends to bring?

each month leading up to this one
has catalyzed in me
an awakening:
sometimes rude,
sometimes enlightening

in attempting authenticity
I put my bare soul forth
in its entirety
only to have it be rejected
for minor parts being different
as if that were a calamity

I welcome the birds and spring
and in turn, they welcome me

> nature can be a better friend
> than wolves in sheep's clothing
> at least you can see what's coming
> *I now see*

A CENTERED VIEW

FELICITOUS SIMPLICITY

not everyone whose attention you desire
can handle your fire
avoid such a situation: the one so dire
your dignity is not for hire

a curious satisfaction feels attached to my current age
so, not with time rewound
but just for a brief moment I'd want again to be *fifteen*

where a simple look,
a word
smile on the face,
or an awkward, blushing embrace

it was everything

it still is…

                    we just forget it with all the social ambition… *in between*

'A Homemaker is Already a Teacher AND Nurse to Her Kids'

It's true, dear reader. No, not necessarily the title of this section in its entirety. Rather, that I quote this because I was indeed told this by that AK Party-member guy friend of mine. The one of a traditional-mindset in Turkey whom I mentioned in the previous Section.

Upon being unable to find paid, local work out of graduate school in 2008 (right at the onset of the financial crash which affected New York City immensely), I obtained certification in T.E.S.O.L (Teaching English to Speakers of Other Languages). Subsequently, I went to my birth city of Istanbul to teach- thinking I'd be more successful with it there. I would often discuss my 'grandiose' dreams of eventually becoming a college instructor and writer with my friend.

He'd tell me I was working 'too hard' for 'nothing'. That I was 'attractive', and hence did not 'have to' do so. That I could meet someone who'd be the main breadwinner so I could then use my 'hobbies' of teaching and writing with my future children- as my 'purpose' in life, having been born a woman. Although I would roll my eyes and downplay such thinking as

A CENTERED VIEW

'outdated' because he'd never 'lived abroad' to have his vision 'broadened' enough, privately his words had gotten to me more than I would ever care to admit.

"Why am I going on all these unfruitful job interviews, feeling depleted- when I see scantily-clad women with rich husbands at restaurants, whom I know aren't working full-time?" I'd ponder to myself. *"Maybe my friend is right. Maybe I really do have to dress either like those women, or cover-up as a fashionable 'hijabi' to 'land' a wealthy, government-supported husband, and spend my weekends organizing fancy dinners rather than pulling my hair out over a laptop…"*

I can go into the next 'catalyst' sequences of events and details of my life that led me to eventually giving another long-term guy friend a romantic 'chance'- namely my daughter's father, Kemal, and marry him to live with him in Norway where I would then spend most of my time writing my first novel. But, alas, you can read between the lines anyway, dear reader. Besides, this is not a general autobiography. I'm no famous celebrity to need one, and nor do I aspire to be. If I can continue to inspire and entertain readers, that's enough for me.

Yet I mention it because that era in my life (my mid-twenties) was an eye-opening symbol for something I'd come across several times in my life:

triggers for change. Rejection causing redirection. Poor timing becoming a catalyst in changing my plans. Heartbreaks and disappointments causing me to close those 'doors' and open others to new professional opportunities and romantic chances.

Needless to say, I never ended up being like any of the aforementioned group of women, and certainly did not marry a necessarily 'wealthy' husband. But Kemal, God bless him, was more 'abundant' in love and character than any men I'd met, and I'll always be thankful for our union and, of course, its fruit- our daughter.

There's always a certain excitement in youth over 'future possibilities', isn't there? Who will you marry? What will your career consist of? How will your children be, if you even have any? And then, you grow up. You get the answers to those things. And then come your mid 30's- hitting you hard. You're faced with the inevitability of aging and less enthusiasm, despite a wiser and more self-appreciating soul. 'Ironic' was always my least favorite Morisette song, and 'Catch 22' my most feared Joseph Heller novel.

Speaking of ironies, let's examine the following. I've always been a creative soul inhabiting a body born into a realism-inclined, fixed-mindset family (if you've never checked out Carol S. Dweck's book *Mindset*, I use it in one of the Business English courses I teach and would definitely recommend it). My choice of major in Political Science in college was mainly to please my parents- especially my mom, who warned me not only that there wouldn't be 'money' for me to make in creative endeavors, but that I'd end up meeting 'predator' men in such fields.

As you've read, dear reader- I, of course, ended up meeting more 'predators' during my daily school life and political internships than in creative fields. I ended up never earning a dime off of politics- instead making a living off of creative writing and- randomly- teaching. I studied Politics for 6 years- graduate studies included- never to work in it, but 'ironically' to have my marriage fall victim to it after the events of July 15, 2016 in Turkey.

I have to give it to my mother though- when she's on point, she's on point. As aforementioned: she, too, like many among her generation growing up in Istanbul, had struggled with dichotomies. She knew I enjoyed performing theatrical monologues in school, and would often tell me that 'politics' was 'similar to acting' since it too would put people in 'public positions' and required 'charisma'. (Yeah- she's had her occasional 'creativity-supporting' moments, in hindsight).

When I mainly ended up teaching language for a living- working as such for over a decade now- I gave her another analogy, instead. "Not politics, mom, but, rather-*teaching* has become 'like acting' for me," I told her. "For not only can I 'perform' in front of a classroom as my 'stage' to make lessons more interesting for students- but I could thus also be able to inspire people in general, just as actors do."

My epiphany ended up being this: I'd originally warmed up to politics (and even had inspired to go into acting) for the deeper purpose and calling I ultimately ended up finding in teaching and writing. Namely, the one of *inspiring people*.

It took me over a decade to arrive here at the point I'm at now. I'm certainly not famous, but I do feel somewhat influential- especially after having received so much heartwarming feedback on my writing from readers, as well as on my teaching skills from anonymous student surveys. Life truly became what ended up happening when I'd been 'busy making other (academic and professional) plans', indeed, as that saying goes.

Yet, strangely, I wouldn't have had it any other way. Like an actress, in a way, I got the chance to play various 'roles' in life, and feel fulfilled having had no regrets and 'what ifs'. I felt like a diplomat interning at the United Nations, and like a politician while running for my local Democratic primary race. I felt like an actress during acting classes as well

A CENTERED VIEW

as in front of my classrooms at times with certain livelier lessons. I felt like a 'fancy' lady who 'lunches' during various charity events with my mother in her Turkish-American civil society circle, as well as during my role as a military wife- attending fancy balls and tea parties both in NATO surroundings in Europe as well as in Turkey.

The one thing I never would have wanted to become, of course, was my current role as a 'prison wife'. Being that Kemal is a political victim who is imprisoned along with thousands in Turkey without a crime, the term was initially bothersome to me. Yet I've since come to not only accept it, but also appreciate the fact that it's allowed me to empathize with numerous women across the world (and even here in the United States) who also believe fully in the innocence of their incarcerated loved ones and wait for them while struggling to work, go on and remain strong for their children.

Such women and I can add one another on social media and support one another, for example, without ever having met. Knowing we 'get it'- even if we never privately message one another or even engage in any dialogue to do so. Our paths may have never physically crossed, nor our ideologies or backgrounds, but in that realm of being fellow facers of injustice: we become allies, sisters. Even men who've met my husband at one point in their lives have become my virtual brothers- expressing their positive memories with him as well as faith in his innocence. In fact, I've faced more kindness from strangers than some of my so-called friends during this time. At a time when my faith in my home country had started declining, my faith in humanity pulled me back up to the light of human oneness. No matter what happens after this point in our political and legal struggles, I hope to never lose that.

This brings me to another irony. I'd spent most of my 20's trying to avoid becoming an 'ordinary' homemaker of a woman- mostly to make my family and circle 'proud' somehow- only to now be working from home and being just that for the most part. The coronavirus pandemic exacerbated that too, of course. And I'm aware that I wasn't the only 'professional' woman to suddenly have had to become everything to their kids at home. So, had my friend had a point after all? I was, if you think about it, now the owner of high-level diplomas whilst literally being a 'teacher and nurse' to my child at home.

I was also being both a mother and a father to Dalya. I was talking to her mostly in English (since I didn't want her to be confused in school) and it is also the language I express myself best in, while her grandmother was trying to exert more Turkish influence. I had the additional responsibility on my

A CENTERED VIEW

shoulders of being the main decision maker in her life. I was always juggling. And- perhaps the most ironic of all- I was doing all of this alone, as a single-parent, despite technically being married.

Perhaps if we had still been keeping in touch, that guy friend (who has since gotten married himself) may have said: "See, I told you. You tried so hard to climb the professional ladder, only to end up being at home again." And, interestingly enough, I enjoy it! I've never enjoyed cooking this much in my 20's and even as a newlywed (sorry Kemal). So, perhaps it was the quarantine. Or perhaps it was maturity and motherhood that 'domesticated' me, more than family or any man could.

Maybe this, maybe that.

I'm content still in knowing I have obtained various accolades as *ends* in themselves- not necessarily just as *means* to some 'promised destination' of financial abundance that tends to be culturally-pledged for 'successful business women' in Western societies. I'm content in being an example for my daughter and all youth in general. For me, hence, the struggle has been *worth it*.

The *joy of being in that 'flow' and of doing* the studying, applying, networking…sometimes even sacrificing sleep all night in front of a computer. Without any immediate payment or professional success of any kind. I can still be content in knowing that I've been in the 'flow' of laboring purely for the sake of a *struggle*. A struggle that strangely provides joy, in the knowledge that creating is something I love doing. Even if that struggle only rewards me one day out of 29 others in a given month- the immense and pure joy I'd feel in that one day would somehow always be worth it.

I had tried. I had worked hard to improve myself, if for nothing else- *for* myself. For the mere satisfaction of knowing I tried. Like a recipe one can never quite get just right the first time they use it to bake something- but the end result eventually ends up being absolutely delicious, sometimes even when least expected.

When the struggle has become habit- so routine that one random day, success surprises you. The pride you feel in yourself becomes worth every drop of blood, sweat, and tears. You've *experienced*. You've *transformed*. You've *inspired*. You've attuned yourself with your inherent *flow:* whether it be the genetic flow of characteristics acquired from your familial/ethnic bloodline, or the one of your soul obtained from your environment and upbringing.

You haven't merely survived on earth another day. You've *lived*.

A CENTERED VIEW

Self-Identity: As the 'Other' in Various Settings

In my poetry, as well as my semi-autobiographical novels, I've noticed that I often somehow end up talking about *duality*.

Now, mind you, I didn't always feel as clearly-torn between dual cultures-50/50- as I currently do. I want to say that from the age of around 8 years old- when I first arrived in the US- until my teen years, I somehow felt 'more Turkish' than I did during my high school years. That becoming a teenager later 'Americanized' me, with various trends that all teenagers tend to stereotypically be influenced by. But I can't do so. I cannot be wholly honest with myself or with you, dear reader, if I simplify things as clear-cut as that.

The truth is- when I'd arrived here, I was a blank slate. I'd had no real 'strong' sense of 'Turkishness' instilled in me as a child in Istanbul. Instead, family drama following my father's departure from the house and my parents' ensuing divorce had taken precedence over cultural celebrations that would have possibly deepened my identity as 'Turkish' in my early childhood.

SET FREE YOUR FLOW

Ironically, in fact, I never quite even felt 'Turkish' until this fact was pointed out to me by all the other immigrants and 'Americans' in NY. Just as a child really has no racially 'different' concept of skin color until society and life experiences show them the sad dichotomy (I've seen firsthand how my daughter- who equally plays with a variety of dolls- treats skin color simply as the difference between one classmate, for example, having blue eyes while another has brown). I too had no sense of 'Turkishness' until I was 'gobble gobble' teased in elementary school. I had also not celebrated 'Turkishness' in any way until my teen years found me being 'Miss Turkey' twice in annual parades, and hosting shows my mother's women's organization would organize to raise money for a weekend Turkish school (Turkish Women's League of America and its *Ataturk/ Cumhuriyet* school branches, respectively)

Yet on some days, it got (and still does) harder than others. The earliest memory I have, in fact, of my being 'different' is from what must have been around 4th grade- one year after I had emigrated here with my mother. In Turkish culture, we customarily kiss friends and family members on both cheeks to say *hello*, *goodbye*, or even as an affectionate and non-verbal way of saying 'cheer up'. The latter is exactly what I tried to do when I noticed that one of the first friends I had made in school- an Asian girl named Anna (who had language issues as well, so we got along in class)- was sad one day during our cafeteria lunch at P.S. 13 in Queens. I'd asked her what was wrong (or I thought I did, with my limited English at the time), and she just continued to shed some tears. And so, as her classmate and friend, I tried to make her feel better in the 'Turkish' way I then knew how: I gave her a kiss on both cheeks. (Oh, the post-Covid world horror of this if it were to happen now!).

She was stunned, but more so by what ensued almost immediately after I had done so. I'm not sure how those mere fourth graders had heard of the term- and why they were using it as something derogatory- but suddenly one boy yelled 'lesbian!'. Subsequently, almost the entire table was laughing at me. I, of course, had never heard of the term and had no idea what it'd meant- and neither did most of those other children who were laughing, I imagine. But this one boy was- I guess, in retrospect- the 'popular guy' in the class, and I'm sure they must have supposed that if he were teasing someone regarding something, it must indeed have been something *tease-worthy*. And so- they laughed along with him.

Imagine the horror of my mother and stepfather when I returned home that day (I'll now refer to them as my 'parents', as my biological father ceased being one to me along with the divorce when I was 5, though he was alive on this planet until I was nearly 25 years old). "What is a *lesbian,* daddy?" I asked my stepdad, as he was, naturally, the one with the English skills, having grown up in the US himself. I don't recall exactly what he responded, but I remember a lot of curious questions. *Where did you hear that? Who said that?*

Anna, needless to say, felt shy to talk to me following that incident: likely fearing being teased for a mysterious reason for both of us. I was lucky to then develop a friendship with a more outgoing ELL student (English Language Learner in academic terms) named Nicole, of Chilean origin. In Junior High School, it would often follow in this same pattern: I tended to develop friendships with ELL students more than 'American' students, although, to be fair, there were also a lot of 'immigrant' students in the Queens public schools I attended!

The only other Turkish student I ever met was 'Özlem' in junior high school, and we ended up having a tumultuous on again/off again friendship right through our college years. I only mention her here for this following purpose: I learned that meeting other 'Turks' in a 'foreign' city didn't equate to automatically-close friendships. (Interestingly, neither did meeting a couple of other 'Americans' I met in Istanbul when I lived there as a single woman to teach English).

And yet I'd often mistakenly think they would. In my contemporary musings about the woes of social categorizations,

A CENTERED VIEW

I find that, in retrospect, I'd been so conditioned to them that not only was I a victim of categorizations, but also a perpetrator myself in terms of my expectations.

I wasn't the only one. Over the years I met many Turks living in New York who told my family and I the same thing. How they'd end up creating 'smoke breaks' and 'car rides' and basically any opportunity just to talk to someone in Turkish for socialization- even people they'd never previously see themselves chatting up due to differences in lifestyles.

Turkish or not, I tended to get along with male friends better growing up and had trouble with female friendships lasting beyond the periodic commonalities I referred to earlier. Furthermore, I also ended up hurt by friends of my own cultural background more frequently: with some sort of dramatic fall-out playing out, in contrast to a subtle fading of non-Turkic friendships.

Aside from personality clashes and losing the test of time (surely experienced across the world): I would, in hindsight, attribute my particular friendships woes to unclear categorizations. I loved to dance in clubs, for example, but had to watch the way I dressed and return home by a certain time. My lack of freedom with my time availabilities and lifestyle choices in general tended to irritate non-Turkish friends who didn't face the same intensity of possessiveness ('protection') from their families. I was neither 'the prude Turkish girl' nor the quintessential 'American party girl'. I was often made to feel, in fact, that I wasn't 'cool' enough to for the cooler parties, yet also not the favorite among more traditional Turkish friends to hang out with (especially with their boyfriends around the same social settings as us). The idea that I genuinely loved dancing and music- and that I honestly was not looking to flirt with anyone- would never occur to them. A girl enjoying dancing for the art of it- after all- is a more 'American' thing. I'd feel extremely misunderstood and misjudged, and this hurt me more than by any non-Turkish friend doing so; the shock felt double-fold, somehow.

    I also acquired my sense of being not only Turkish or American, but by that point equally *Turkish-American* in my college years, as I experienced stigmas attached to 'Turkishness' with regards to controversial historic events. From Armenian-American protesters at the annual Turkish parade (to whom I'd wave conciliatorily as the parade 'queen'), I heard of the term 'genocide' for the first time, and genuinely wondered 'why do they hate us when we don't hate them?'. From my stepdad's professional circle of Greek-American colleagues and friends, I heard of the term (with their half- jokes and possessive sentiments about modern-day 'Istanbul') 'Constantinople' for the first time.

A CENTERED VIEW

From college friendships in general, I only heard 'stereotypes' against which I'd continuously need to battle and defend. "No, camels aren't common in Turkey: we're *not* an Arabic nation made of deserts". "No, women *can* walk outside at night, and are not forced to cover their hair". "No, we cannot be labeled as a third-world country- we have the second largest military in NATO, don't you know!?"

Finally, I must include the following addendums to the issue of friendships resulting from periodic commonalities- for they often tend to be pronounced with Turkish friendships in particular. Commiserating and nosiness.

MINI-SCENARIO:

Friend A: **Hey, *canım*** (Turkish equivalent of 'honey'). **Oh my God,** (insert name of some 'heartbreaker'**) didn't take me out again this weekend. I definitely think he's seeing someone. How about** (insert the name of the other friend's heartbreaker)**? Has he finally been attentive to you this weekend?**

Friend B: **Aww, I'm sorry to hear that, canım. I was just about to call you!** (no, they weren't). **Well, yes, actually. He surprised me with flowers and took me to a nice dinner.**

Friend A: Oh. Oh, nice. Happy for you. That's great! (::disappointed sigh:

Misery indeed can love company as part of human nature across all nationalities, yes, but only Turkish-American friends in particularly would make me feel guilty somehow if I suddenly became happy when they were still sad. Or, adversely, turn their backs on me when my luck in life appeared to take a turn for the worse at a particular time. Coldness flourished as text messages diminished. I deemed myself a friend for people to share despair- a *'kötu gün dostu'* in Turkish. They didn't seem to want or be able to handle me when I was doing well, nor wanted to make the effort for me anymore when they themselves were. To those fair-weather acquaintances I'd mistakenly called friends: I'm letting them go with love. They can go rob another person's aura without paying with genuine friendship.

Didn't anyone tell them we were all on the same roller coaster in life- that there is never some underlying competition? Didn't anyone tell them, just as importantly, that just because I was going through a rougher period in my life than they were, and needed to vent, I was never going to stay in the 'dumps' for long- and that they didn't need to lose their faith in my value as a person to somehow be effort-worthy enough to keep in their lives? Would they have been so fickle had they been true friends? All I know is, I've been hurt just as much by platonic friendships in my life as romantic ones. And my cultural duality, for my aforementioned reasons, definitely often felt like it had played a major part in it.

As for nosiness- I think the term speaks for itself. I never experienced a string of questions that my American side would deem 'intrusive' as frequently as I have by Turks. *'How much?' 'Why? What's the size? What's the label? What's his salary? Which school? Which restaurant/hotel- how many stars?'.* There's almost no question too 'personal' in general in Turkish culture (under the guise, of course, of 'making friendly conversation').

Yet, once again, I've come to witness how bicultural Turkish-Americans like myself have tended to be this way more than others. After I was interviewed by a Turkish-American online news website about my premier novel, for instance, I noticed how- aside from a couple of genuinely warm and congratulatory social media comments- the rest ended up indeed being judgmentally intrusive ones by fellow Turks residing in the US. *"What's the name of her publishing company- is it one of the mainstream ones?"* ("What does it matter?" I wanted to respond, but didn't.) This nosiness- tinged with a touch of both arrogance and pressure of putting on 'appearances'- has, in my opinion, had a detrimental effect on Turkish-American lobby groups not being as politically effective as the ones of other cultural minorities in the US (whose groups don't focus on the 'categorizations' of their various organizations, uniting instead for a common cause for their people's benefit).

In *The Catalyst,* I intrinsically found myself gravitating toward the theme of environmental friendships as well. In case you haven't read my romantic suspense novel yet (what are you waiting for?), here is a brief summary of one of the underlying themes as it pertains to this particular section. Kaitlin Maverick, the female protagonist of the story, feels so alone and desperate for friendships in a new land she's traveled to through marriage, she signs up for social activities she's not even interested in just to have human company (other than sales associates on various shopping outings to pass the time while her husband is at work). Was this portion taken from my direct life experience? You can bet it most certainly was.

Subsequently, the reader ultimately sees how everyone Kaitlin has met crossed paths with her for a reason- as 'catalysts' to motivate her to take a certain step in her life she otherwise wouldn't have. Her feelings of jealousy over a friendly female colleague of her husband, for example, incites her to join a social club- where she meets a Turkish woman named Sibel, who herself turns out to be a 'catalyst' for her of another kind.

Situational and environmental friendships of convenience may have been just for that, in retrospect,

A CENTERED VIEW

for many of us: for catalysis to make certain changes in our lives or open our minds to some things we otherwise never would have.

That annoying colleague who convinced you to quit a steady job on Wall Street? You may have gotten angry with her- but ultimately you may have henceforth redirected your life in another professional direction more suited for you (autobiographical, yes). That frenemy with whom you were seemingly 'close' one week and distant the next? Think about it. Did they incite a recognition in you- even if it was ultimately self-recognition or truth-facing you otherwise may have been too scared to admit even to yourself? Yup. You've guessed it. They were catalysts for your life.

Am I saying that literally everyone we meet is for some grand reason? That random parent, for instance, with whom you conversated about the weather while waiting to pick up your kids from their pre-K class? No. Not at all. However, if the same parent did happen to mention- even if casually so during the few conversations you may have had- that their kid was enjoying a certain ballet class, for example, which made you realize your own daughter was inclined to do the same? Exactly- they could have been catalysts.

SET FREE YOUR FLOW

The Reclusive Open-Book

My general shyness growing up wasn't really any more noteworthy than the shyness, I'm sure, employed by millions of people around the world. Perhaps that number is even smaller in scale if I were to include myself in a group of those who were shy children due to an absentee parent. Adding the final characteristic of shyness due to having emigrated into a whole new country as a child with your mother and her new husband? Now we may be getting somewhere: I may truly be in a smaller category of people with similar experiences (if you, dear reader, are one such person- kindly contact me to briefly share your story as well. I'm genuinely curious).

Not only had I never been able to ride a bike (perhaps for psychological reasons, due to the story I shared in Section 1) but I barely remember having done many other typically 'childish' things either. I was already an only child. I never remember uttering the word for 'father' in my first language of Turkish- 'baba'. I never grew up playing various games with any cousins. With various lingual barriers here in New York on top of that, I felt so lonely at one point, in fact, that I remember having told the 2,3 friends I was able to make in grade school that I had a mysterious brother and sister (no, not imaginary friends, as I was well aware I was technically lying). I had no idea really why I felt I had to do so, either. I even remember inviting some over for Halloween trick-or-treating in my apartment. When they'd asked about the whereabouts of my so-called 'siblings', I had to tell them one was 'away in college' while another was 'off somewhere shooting hoops'.

Ironically, life would show me perhaps I was already embodying what my subconscious already knew I was- an older sister to a half-brother being raised across the pond in England, also without knowing about me, and also sour about the man who'd fathered us both.

That's right, dear reader. I hope you can tell by this point that- with that kind of an imagination- I could have either gone on to develop serious mental issues, or turn to art as survival. Luckily, I found solace ultimately in writing, and chose the latter.

There I was. Shy to say 'hi' to people I knew on the street sometimes, yet completely 'at home' whenever an opportunity to 'prove myself' presented itself as a schoolgirl-

especially in the form of creativity. A school play? The school Chorus? The spelling bee? A poetry contest? I was there.

"Damn girl," I remember one particular high school classmate telling me after one of our senior play rehearsals. "You dance well and you're not shy at all! I wasn't expecting that from you! It's always the shy ones, isn't it…"? Surprising people who would later express that they'd initially expected me to be shy or aloof (or even sometimes 'snobby' and- gulp- 'bitchy') would always motivate me.

I had to not only overcome the loneliness I felt in my family life and cultural duality, but also this 'false' image I quickly became aware that I was displaying to people. In retrospect, even in photographs I see that I barely smiled as a schoolgirl- even though I'm pretty sure I thought I was doing so.

Subsequently in my life, I felt so afraid of being misunderstood among both Turks and Westerners ("I can't stay out late, but I still love to party"/ "I physically can't handle fasting during Ramadan but I'm still very spiritual and believe in our prayers and alms-giving") that I decided somewhere along the line to be an *open-book*.

Despite my overprotective mother always warning me against my tendency to overshare every detail of my life with friends and acquaintances- being anything other than an open book eventually became difficult. If I didn't overshare, I'd feel

A CENTERED VIEW

'mistakenly categorized'. And despite Western self-help quotes everywhere telling us, 'don't care what others think'- I did. I cared what they thought- not because I wanted to mold my life choices in accordance with others' opinions, but rather to balance my idealist individuality with a dose of such 'realism'.

Did *The Catalyst*, for instance, require its subtly-erotic scene toward the end? Artistically- for the storyline- it absolutely did. Could I have described it with longer, more evocative wording than the sentence or two I ended up using to describe it? Not if I didn't want to completely ostracize Turkish readers (and my own family) whom I knew would be reading it.

You can sell hundreds of books and even thousands. You can be complimented on just about every part of your being you can imagine. You can physically be in a glorious space in a glorious town, with glorious belongings. You can receive 50 likes or 500 on social media. Ultimately it all comes down to this: are you smiling as you fall asleep? If you are unable to maintain meaningful connections in this life, you're lonely even if not alone. Period.

With my daughter Dalya, it has been really fascinating to watch her grow up in the United States, from a younger age than I did. Watching her daily struggles with shyness in greeting new people that belie the artistic and 'outgoing-with-familiar-people' side of her, it feels like watching a movie clip of my own life: right before my very eyes. It is as if God is giving me a second chance in life. A do-over of my childhood, through my daughter. Not for her to 'accomplish what I couldn't', as that parental cliché goes, but rather to purposely view the world through a child's excited eyes- more than I was able to as a child.

which of your shadows represents your true essence best
as you stride?
are you able to swim and ride the waves of the highest tide
you experience inside?
you're still that young girl with the messy handwriting
pretending
in mock interviews that she's already written the books she's
discussing
you're still the hider of the most precious jewels lurking in your
imagination
while also the writer whose low mood rises
when it can motivate another:
an over-sharer
no need to have all the answers
or feign divinity
no need to be anything other than humanly free
imperfectly perfect
just BE

A CENTERED VIEW

Many of my English students share that one of the most surprising facets of Americans according to them has been rhetorical questions. "Americans ask how everyone is doing without really expecting an answer," they say. It's true. But I could never become 'that' American. If someone asks me 'how are you?'- I pretty much verbally-vomit various details of my day. And I truly believe that I've been doing so- now in both hindsight as well as self-reflection- in order to wholly be myself. So that I can increase the chance of somehow being recognized by my 'soul tribe'- friends that would find my 'weirdness' and 'quirkiness' compatible with their own. No matter which socio-cultural 'categorization' we were boxed in. No matter which 'group' we belonged to.

As Marilyn Monroe is attributed as once upon a time saying: "I knew I belonged to the world, not because I was very talented or even beautiful, but because I never belonged anywhere else." *Belonging.* Can someone missing a parent growing up ever truly feel like they belong somewhere? Could I have made wiser dating choices- and perhaps better friendships- if my birth father had validated me? I will never know.

"why did you leave me?"
a tearful voice asked through the phone receiver
there would never be an answer
he hadn't just left her mother

SET FREE YOUR FLOW

so the girl would always ponder
and never ask the same to another
she can finally understand
now that she's older
and with that answer
will feel broken again by a man
no longer

"I miss you, baba," my daughter now says into the phone receiver. Except this time, unlike me in my own childhood- she isn't speaking into the void. Even if- for over 5 years- it has only been through letters and the occasional/brief telephone message rather than in-person: she knows she has a father somewhere in the world who's dying to hear her voice.

And with even just that, if nothing else, I can get some closure for my own childhood. I can make peace with my own experience: know that my daughter is accepted, in a way I was never able to feel. I hope this ultimately can lead to an increased sense of both self-acceptance and self-confidence in her later years growing up, with her friendships and all relationships as well. Sometimes, I feel I even went through these things so I can be there for my daughter in a more understanding and helpful way when she goes through similar things in her life.

A CENTERED VIEW

purity is enough
your peace of mind
is enough
to not only accept being alone
but actually relish it
treasure it
make the most of it

never lonely, even when alone
much lovelier now, than with any fake clone
of the lost that had been- and could only be
the only one to really feel like home
we can become grown
better on our own

little one

remember your wings are not meant to carry and hold
the burdensome weight of ungrateful, additional load

if you give them the flashlight to use on a whim
to create shine around their dark souls
to use and dispose
who is going to help you when you need your own light
back to carry you through?
when you were counting on them to shine for you too

wisdom, I'm afraid, only pays a visit
when you've had enough, reached your limit

SECTIONAL ANECDOTES

Growing up bi-culturally has meant:

- choosing a Major based on an 'ideal' profession it could lead to, deemed as such by your social-circle. Where the question of 'what job would make you happy?' is an absurd and almost unheard one. *"Her daughter will be studying Business? Good money. Oh, teacher? Nice- men like feminine jobs like teachers and nurses. Teachers also have more days off to rear children easier. MY niece is studying Art. Argh! She'll never land a good job, nor a wealthy and respectable man…"*

-being told to come out of your comfort zone and 'go say hi' to potential 'friends' or 'professional contacts' deemed appropriate by one's circle. My mother once convinced me to approach Rahmi Koç on a Turkish Airlines flight, to let him know I 'idolized his company' (I didn't even know what they did) and that I'd been looking for a job fresh out of graduate school (that part was true). He gave me his card to e-mail my CV, saying he appreciated my 'go-getter' attitude. I did land a fancy interview in Istanbul 2 weeks after that- one that, of course, went nowhere.

- Expressing 'extroverted' qualities most comfortably through *art*. A microphone or social platform allowed me to make myself 'heard'- and feel accepted- despite nervousness.

THE WARRIOR

you carry the sword
to fight uphill battles
of injustice
both real and imaginary

the burden is heavy
generational responsibility

break the proverbial curse
free the repressed verse

write out your world into existence
protagonist of your own art: fight and employ persistence

slay the dragon
of fearing what others think

don't forget that your sword
is the one that bleeds ink

SET FREE YOUR FLOW

GAMBIT

they copy you
but it's not the same
no room for a princess
in this game

I've got Knights and Bishops
on my side
you've only got insufficient Pawns
and your pride

a spiritless face falls flat on a screen
it's obvious who's the original Queen
the previous efforts: I appreciate
but it's history now: I won't take the bait

Checkmate

DO BEFORE DONE

flutter off
before discovering your plight

you've been set free
before prepared for flight

remember you're a butterfly
not a used kite

Section IV: Flowing Through Parenting

POETIC POLITICS
(STUDENTS OF POLITICS BECOME ITS VICTIMS)

THE MENDING OF UNBANDAGED WOUNDS

a man
politically-imprisoned
kept away from his wife, his
child, his home, his human
dignity
crime-free
he is joined by many
similar victims of circumstance
for company

'he'll soon be set free,' they say
'we live in a democracy- it can't
forever stay this way'

is the path toward mending a
probability or simply a distant
possibility?
to repair the shattered
backbone of a nation once
promising the ideal regional
legality,
when many have bent their
backbones cramped into
caged-spaces meant for a few,
not twenty?

is there a path
to ameliorate and heal
families back together
up ahead?

following
tears of widowed wives and
orphaned children,
not of ghosts, but of the
living dead?

every evening, for all of them
filled with excruciating dread?

animals can lick their wounds
in place of bandages
what can separated families do,
when faced with human
savages?

TWO LITTLE GIRLS

I wish I could tell her it all gets better, when you love yourself enough
to better yourself …through any weather

wish I could tell her - if they step on you to rise
or play you for a fool, leaving you misled
you'll be the one in the end more wise
and you'll always be one step ahead

don't wrap your entire life
around being someone's wife
anything can end
always need an alternate plan

ours was torn by our birth state
some other marriages are slashed by hate
or losing the one the other cannot appreciate

wish I could tell her … you'll rise through the tears
you're more than your fears…wise beyond your years

to the little girl

both the pure one I see by me
and the one I see still in the mirror

SET FREE YOUR FLOW

T.A.M (Turkish-American Mothering)

It's largely universal (though there are certainly refreshing stories of exceptions) for parents to 'disapprove' of their offsprings' professional pursuits. It's another thing, unfortunately, for Turkish-American ones (or perhaps bicultural parents in general) to do so. Because when they do, they not only point to the usual and universal parental 'concerns' over one's ability to earn enough to make a living or the potential dangers associated with a certain job, but rather also tend to lead to quarrelsome and judgmental accusations.

Imagine someone that can list an entire set of 'terrible' things about your choices- but then back off into a safety net of *"...but it's only because I think you deserve better"* or, *"I'm not saying to leave them/change your mind. I won't take that responsibility. I'm just saying...It's up to you."* That's likely a Turkish-American parent. Refer to this following sketch for my case and point.

Mother: **What are you doing?**

The son/daughter: **I'm painting, mom.**

A CENTERED VIEW

Mother: **Don't you have real work to do? Why don't you look for some real work online? You're wasting too much time on your hobbies. Look at ……** (insert name of random family acquaintance's son or daughter)

The son/daughter: **But, mom, this is my dream and I can actually make a living with this as well. Be a little more open-minded, please. This makes me happy.**

Mother: **Will you be happy when you're a bum on the street, unable to pay your rent and bills? What will everyone say? You must take after your** (insert 'black sheep' family member's name here). **Why did we work so hard to get you through college? For this? Are you trying to give us a heart attack?**

The son/daughter: **No need to be paranoid just yet, please! I'll always regret it if I don't at least try. Everyone else sees that and supports me on this, I don't understand how you…**

Mother: **…This is for your good! Your friends aren't going to be honest and warn because they want the best for you. They see you as a rival- of course they don't want you to become more successful than them.**

The son/daughter: **…Right. And just what is your definition of 'success'?**

SET FREE YOUR FLOW

Mother: **…That's enough. Just wrap it up quick- you still have to help me out with these boxes.**

End scene.

Allow me to share an even more subjective and concrete example from my own personal experience, dear reader. Though my mother likes to refute it to this day, she's the reason I chose Political Science as my college major: a major which hasn't helped me professionally thus far in any way, shape or form.

Now, fair is fair. She *does* have a point when she says that, yes, at 18-19 I could have indeed taken responsibility for my decision, I suppose (in retrospect). And, I do. Yes: I made the decision to major in Political Science. Yet it was done so with so much maternal influence exerted that I cannot tell where the line of 'interference' ended and my 'personal decision-making' began. An influence that externally gazed upon my physical presence amongst Turkish-American civil society- and likened my presence as 'belonging' in that company- without actually asking me if I was enjoying diplomatic discussions over weekend-cocktails at the Embassy building, munching on little meatballs on toothpicks being passed around by caterers.

A CENTERED VIEW

I also never realized I could have even *had* a 'personal choice' to take on such a responsibility; I was expected to be 'Americanized' and 'individualistic' when it suited the flow of events, whereas mostly I was otherwise expected to be as 'Turkish' and 'family-centric' as possible.

Before starting to write *The Catalyst* in Norway- I had actually started a blog named 'The Musings of a Reluctant Housewife' soon after I'd gotten married and literally had become one (namely, a 'reluctantly' domesticated 'housewife'). *The Catalyst* itself, in fact, had initially had the working title of *Scandal-avia*. (Cheesy, I'm aware, but, hey, in my defense it *does* involve a culturally 'scandalous' plotline taking place in Scandinavia, and I love a good play on words, so…)

On that blog, I'd added some pretty pictures of Norway alongside my first attempts at baking brownies and trying horseback riding; all up until I lost interest as soon as the then newly-rising Instagram proved more 'instantly' satisfying.

Now interestingly enough, even prior to that blog, I used to have another blog named 'T.A.P', which stood for 'Turkish-American Princess'. (I suppose blogging was there for lonely creatives like me before social media really blew up like it has now). I had been chosen twice as the 'Turkish-American princess' in annual parades held in Manhattan- mostly because I was seen as the *hanım hanımcık* ('lady-like') daughter of my

SET FREE YOUR FLOW

Turkish-American non-profit community 'notable' of a mother, and had hence thought that title to be *cute*.

Today, I stand here (well I'm technically sitting and typing these words as I watch the raindrops from my suburban window, dear reader) as a politically-single mother. Trying to 'write out' my 'drops' and creative 'flow' of consciousness in various states of exhaustion. Just like I've been doing whenever I found the chance to type them out after my toddler managed to fall asleep only around midnight. Mostly munching on sour-candy to stay awake (sorry, wisdom teeth).

No 'Musings'. No 'T.A.P'. Perhaps if I didn't go into becoming an author, I could have dabbled in this latest stage in my life using some variation or play on words relevant to my contemporary struggles ('PSM and PMS', perhaps? Get It? *Politically-Single Mother* and…yeah. You get the drift).

What would I have done if Instagram hadn't been there to distract me from delving into typing out all the trauma in the form of blogging, by making me turn to artistic expression as catharsis instead? Symbolic photography and stories (which I've called 'visual storytelling') juxtaposed with political/ human rights related hashtags and captions just may have saved me at the time. Particularly during those 4-months when I'd been bound to Istanbul, due to a travel ban placed following my naval officer husband's incarceration.

A CENTERED VIEW

A ban I was only made aware of *after* I was stopped from boarding my flight to the US by officers leading me to the questioning room. My then two-year-old in my arms. Everyone on the line behind me looking at my being prevented from traveling as if I were some criminal on the run.

"I'm an American citizen," I told them politely. "I should be able to travel, regardless of my husband's local case." The clerk had smirked at me. "It doesn't matter if you're also the citizen of Sweden, lady. This is Turkey- and you have Turkish citizenship, too. Only Turkish laws apply here!" (He wasn't kidding. The American embassy of Istanbul I subsequently called told me the same. It was the first time in my life I'd felt the relative powerlessness of my American citizenship abroad, though up to that point I'd witnessed countless people risking everything for such a citizenship).

We'd just paid a 2017 visit to her father in jail. At the time, I had taken that risk, completely comfortable in knowing I'd never gotten myself involved in anything that could be deemed controversial by the state. Just the opposite, in fact. Remember those Turkish-embassy civil society events I mentioned a bit earlier? The ones with the little meatballs being served on toothpicks? Erdoğan, his wife, and countless other AK Party members would frequent them as well (I even have a photograph with Emine Erdoğan , Abdullah Gül, and countless others. I admit that I-*gulp*- even voted for AKP at one time).

Sigh. Back to 'motherhood'.

"Write to Emine Erdoğan," my mother suggested, referring to the authoritarian president's wife. "She's a mother too. I've seen her cry for those Palestinian children on TV. She may sympathize with your story as well."

"She's not going to be given some random personal mail among countless of others, I'm sure, mom," I'd responded, rolling my eyes. So, I went to the 'official' website the state had created for 'legal complaints'. CIMER. And I wrote. To Emine Erdoğan. To Erdoğan himself. And- yes- out of desperation for my crimeless husband to be released, I wrote even to *him*: the womanizing, skirt-lifting minister himself.

I swallowed my pride as a young woman after the humiliation in his office I'd chosen to ignore, and asked him to help my innocent husband. "Write *him*, too" my mother had further suggested, after all. I didn't tell her. Just like he knew I wouldn't. His position of power and closeness to Erdoğan having given him some sort of protective shield he's since been able to use to overcome various other controversies in the country as well (hushed quickly in the state-influenced media).

I didn't want my mother to become further disappointed with one more 'civil society/political star' amongst our Turkish-American circle. I couldn't do that to her. I had to let her think her social circle still could have some soft power to 'save the day'. Once again: my Turkishness, encouraged by my mother and observation of similar mothers of friends I was witnessing around me, was whispering into my consciousness that influential contacts could 'save the day' in a time of need. My American side had learned by then that that was all BS- and that we can only ultimately really save ourselves. The only thing 'they' were able to 'influence' and 'save' for me had been business-class seats on Turkish Airlines flights and popular concert tickets in Istanbul (That's right. More things of only showiness value).

Now let's move on to: *'Catalysis'*

Yes, I've mentioned my mother's at times overbearing influence- but I've also learned not to blame her. Especially since the birth of my own catalyst: my daughter.

It's easy for a mother of any background to unknowingly 'cross the line' of interfering in a child's life due to a self-made mission of lifetime 'protection'. But Turkish-American mothering tends to be unique with its involvement of the social circle and the child's 'placement' in it. Ranging from: *"They won't invite you without your husband to accompany you- you'll be deemed a threat for their relationships, being a woman alone"* to *"What will they think if Dalya can't speak two languages fluently when many of their kids are bilingual already?"* And, of course, the ever-dreaded, *"Who will want you now for marriage? They'll only be after your body as a woman- or after your citizenship."*

Yes, dear reader. From a young Turkish-American 'princess' blogger to a 'reluctant housewife' musing in Norway: I have now become a *T.A.P.S.M* ('Turkish-American Politically-Single Mom'). Blogger turned Instagrammer.

But- let's remember- *Catalysis*.

I have also been able to evolve myself beyond my mother's imagination for my social-placement predictions. Through going on- despite everything- for Dalya: I have also gone from dreamer to *author*. A Dreamer to Doer. Pursuer of spontaneous nonchalance to meticulous planner and manifester.

I am not a 'princess' or 'queen'- my life certainly has not become what fairy tales are made of (neither Turkish, or any American ones I've heard of, anyway). That is for sure. Yet- I do have a story. A story of my own. A story with my new partner in life: my daughter. She's been left fatherless and I- husbandless- by the Turkish state. Yet we put on smiles on social media and in real life for memories. For inspiration. For each other. I am a Turkish-American mother, too, now. Imperfect in my own ways. But I am my own. And I aim to inspire my daughter and others like her to have the courage to be able to find their 'own' inherent flow and mission, as well.

A CENTERED VIEW

Before I verbally give the proverbial 'floor' to my politically-jailed husband in the next sub-section, I want to continue this 'parenting' section on a lighter topic, dear reader, to ease into the increasingly more emotional subject matter. As we all know, after all, motherhood is such an easy breezy task to discuss by itself, isn't it? (Cue in the American sarcasm punch line). But, just for a little fun, let's now explore a relatively more humorous aspect of daily parenting life. *Food.* Let's hit it. Bon appétit/ *Afiyet olsun*.

Sincerely,

T.A.P.S.M.A

(Turkish-American Politically-Single Mom, and Author)

SET FREE YOUR FLOW

Pekmez versus Avocadoes

In Turkey, there's a saying: '*Anasına bak, kızını al*', which roughly translates to 'look at the mother when buying the daughter'…since of course, in many Eastern traditions, brides are still thought of as being 'bought' into the grooms' families like pieces of furniture.

There's also another saying that goes '*Armut dibine düşer*'. This is a more culturally neutral one since there's a similar one in English about the apple not falling too far from the tree (Well, except, of course for the Turkish version mentioning pears instead of apples. Perhaps because more Turkish women have pear-shaped bodies like mine? Who knows? I smile. I digress). Why is this relevant, you may ask? (No. Not the 'pear' joke). Well, it is precisely so since I will now elaborate on the more traditional 'mothering' ways of the generations before mine, in comparison to the newer generations' relatively more 'modernized' practices.

I'm pretty sure there were no avocadoes sold in Turkey when I was being brought up as a baby, but my daughter has sure loved eating them for breakfast ever since I first started giving her solids at around 5 months. 'Avocadoes are packed with just

A CENTERED VIEW

as much nutrition as eggs', numerous parenting blogs and news articles- both Turkish and American- were screaming at me.

Up until becoming a mom, I'd enjoyed avocadoes only as the main ingredients in guacamole: found in numerous diners and Mexican restaurants in New York City. Having tried the fruit itself and gotten no taste- I never thought that something other than the onion-tomatoes-spices combination used to make a good dip for my favorite Tostitos chips could be created for a baby- until the day I came up with one. My then barely 6-month-old baby was deemed to be 'slightly underweight' after my 'breastfeeding' was apparently no longer enough. I was told by her doctor to 'start introducing solid foods earlier than the typical 6-month mark'. In desperation, I began experimenting with different combinations; Dalya ended up loving the taste of avocadoes sweetened with shredded pears, which I combined with shredded walnuts and sometimes almonds (for the extra brain power boost which I'd also read about).

Now, this is not an article on 'Nutrition for your Child'- I would love to be able to write one, but there are already many such wonderful articles written in that subject by mothers and experts more talented in that area than I. So, what's my reason for bringing up avocadoes? Why, no one in Turkey seemed to get me when they'd heard that that's what I'd been giving my baby for breakfast, of course!

Immediately, I received such remarks as, *"...That's nice, but you already give eggs: why the avocado?"*, *"Isn't avocado something that should be given as a fruit snack in between meals rather than for breakfast?"*, and, of course, my favorite- *"Why don't you give her a traditional breakfast of tomatoes and white cheese with olives so she can get used to it? Our classically-Turkish 'Tahin and pekmez'* (tahini and grape molasses) *is better than peanut butter and jelly or jam, you know: and much more filling..."*

There it was: the top three ingredients of a 'typical' Turkish breakfast, thrown in my face. I could have tried to explain as much as I can that my daughter tried but didn't like eating raw tomatoes yet, and that she spit out white cheese and olives each time. I could have even fallen back on my typical 'social commentary loving' self and stated, *"Who's to say what a 'typical' breakfast 'should' be like? It's different all around the world."* But, alas, I just took a deep breath, smiled and said (I still do): *"I tried it all, but this is how my girl likes it, and I'm the only one who can get her to eat* (yes, they had all tried)."

Period. End of discussion.

People ranging from my mother-in-law (with whom I had to live during those entrapped months waiting for either my husband to come home *or* be able to fly back to New York to my family home again- whichever happened first) to neighbors,

A CENTERED VIEW

friends and my own family members. They all judged me slightly in my 'non-traditional' choices for my child in this respect.

What it all comes down to is- what's 'right' is what works for you and your child. You could take a little bit of the East and a little bit of the West, and create a formulaic soup in life that works best for you: no one else has to drink it if they don't like. A little bit of *traditional* choices with a little bit of more *modern* ones- and combining them all to you and your little ones' content. And no one should be able to judge you, since they're neither the ones living your life, nor the ones possibly offering to help in any way (except by offering unsolicited advice). Well-intentioned or not, such interference only tends to contribute mental stress to a mother who is already under tremendous pressure to raise her child as best as she can.

It's not just avocadoes, of course. I also tried to have my daughter be raised with being accustomed to having both the 'American' peanut butter-and-jam combination and the 'Turkish' tahin/pekmez combination on her morning bread slices. I had an Asian neighbor back in New York City tell me her toddler daughter only ate plain rice with fruit juice in the mornings! 'Good for her!'… I'd exclaimed at the time. Who was I to offer any further opinions to a mother who volunteered on her own that she had 'tried everything' but that her daughter had 'refused to eat much of anything else'? As for me? I replaced the 'jam' with 'honey' in the classically-American PB&J combo, The inclusion of 'honey' satisfied 'them', whilst my insistence on the peanut butter 'for protein' satisfied me *and* my delighted daughter, who luckily continues to enjoy this unique combination to this day.

Added to all this has been the stigma that came with the fact that my daughter was, and still is, very attached to me (I breastfed her until, *gulp,* well into her pre-K years, upon her insistence: I believe she insisted for the extra comfort since her dad couldn't be around). This is a girl, if you recall, who doesn't eat white cheese, either. What else could I do? Well, I got her to eat yogurt to compensate for the possible calcium loss, and luckily, she still likes yogurt- so that has worked out okay. I hope.

Being a parent has meant an increase in humility. On your absolute worst day- when you're sleep-deprived, down in the dumps with intrusive, depressive thoughts about yourself and your life- there they are. Adorably innocent and in need of you to be stronger in order to serve and help them in some way. You're 'needed'. And in that depressive moment- you hence feel 'relevant' for a

A CENTERED VIEW

bigger purpose on this earth than making sure your ego feels victorious and accomplished.

Allow me to reference once again, dear reader, the Turkish proverb about the pear. 'Armut dibine düşer'. My mother was wronged by my birth father, and I was 'fatherless' for the couple of years between their divorce and her remarriage.

I wonder now how my daughter will reference her own childhood. Will she focus on her own upbringing by a lone mother? Or will she focus on the difference between the way that that happened as such? Namely, will she dedicate her life to political and legal justice for those wronged like her father was, whereas I have dedicated mine to using creativity to heal my abandonment issues and life experiences?

I wonder if my daughter will *write out* her angst against injustice- witnessing the political and legal one inflicted on her father. Here, dear reader, is the poem 'Blue' in full: written by *my* teenager self. The same one I referenced in my poem 'Innocence Lost' in *Write Out Your Drops.*

SET FREE YOUR FLOW

Blue
I'm blue
there's no end in sight
my mind keeps wandering off to
the different possibilities that
seems so far away and
unattainable
Blue
I'm like a satellite, roaming
around space slow at times and
fast at others; yet I'm all alone in
the vast universe
I can see the planets and other
formations but they are so distant
I'm stuck floating around this
miniscule space called earth
Blue
I'm the frosted flake you're
encircling with your spoon,
drowning me inside
this sour milk
and I can't escape for I am
lifeless- merely grain
I can't protest
Blue
I'm the other side of you
the side that reveals itself when
there is fear, embarrassment or
anger
the world is baby pink then beige
and it seems purple like scars,
then red, black, and red
again...but it is never white
for the only thing pure in life is
death, and this has become my
motto
Blue
I'm stuck on this shadow of
breaths and motions, senses and
emotions

Like Glue

A CENTERED VIEW

Addendum:

General Things I Would Tell the Little Girl Now

First, if someone has chosen another in your place, avoid losing yourself in the paranoia that they're continuously idealizing that person at your expense and relative detriment. Their choice may have been a logical one for societal support and ease, rather than one based on intense attraction or an emotional connection as deep as yours.

Better to be 'the one that got away' and 'what if' rather than 'good riddance'. Accept all 'goodbyes' with grace…for even if it was none of the above (and the new couple is genuinely in love), be sincerely happy for them. Better they met their 'one' now rather than later down the road when it would have been harder for you and have caused you to lose time. Better to be free to find your 'one'- starting with intensifying love and prioritization for yourself.

Second: beautiful and attractive are different things, the latter being subjective. A 'beautiful' person may subliminally be attracted to someone that may be attractive to *them* more than others' eyes can see. Childhood experiences, familial reminders, deeply-buried hobbies and fantasies may be triggered, which may be activated by someone not conventionally considered 'beautiful' or 'handsome'. Thus, 'tis truly best to be your authentic self. For you never know who will be attracted to all the beautiful quirks hidden deep beneath your surface.

Third: Your emotions- just like your individual experiences- are valid. Don't let anyone underestimate what you've been through as "*…oh, you're not the only one…get over it*". Only you- and God above- can truly know what you've experienced behind closed doors.

If you loved someone, for instance: own it. Don't deny it. That love exists – like an offspring formed from love. It's been birthed, and cannot be taken back into the womb. Take the love, even after a relationship is over. Place it upon yourself. Upon your art. Upon someone or some form that deserves it. Use it. Be catalyzed by it. *Write it out. Set it free.* Don't curse it.

Fourth. We live in a world where one's idea of *sin*- obtained from a personal understanding of a particular religion's holy book, and something sacred between the individual and God- will most likely be different than the dogmatic ones more audibly promoted. Among many Islamic societies in particular: one that unnecessarily highlights punishment in the afterlife rather than the Koran-written clemency of God provided through true repentance.

Though it may at times be difficult to do so, we must make an effort not to categorize anyone with automatically-assumed 'labels' or 'traits'. I have encountered genuinely devout Muslim women (whom the world would never deem as such based on their uncovered appearance) commit more charitable acts and pray daily when compared to some of their more 'covered' counterparts. I have also encountered numerous open-minded women in headscarves with higher levels of both education and freedom in their social powers compared to my own self.

Forgive your curious and imaginative mind while keeping your intentions and actions as pure as you can. Do the best you can to be a good, grateful person for this precious life we've been given- and your flow can only be your compass toward a beautiful life experience (where you can enrich others' lives and in turn, enrich your own).

Fifth: my generation growing up didn't have all the tools of the internet and terms for various neuroses as the current one. Beware of *narcissists*, for they can be anywhere and in all forms, sometimes covertly so. You'll surely fall for the hauntingly beautiful Turkish songs on vacations: focus more on their melodies, for most contain 'love-bombing' lyrics that will allow you to believe someone confessing 'love' too early on without it being genuine. Whereas, in the US, such lyrics are so rare that they become controversial (sorry Bruno Mars, to 'ring your ears' once again, as the Turkish saying goes, but I'm thinking of your controversial hit 'Grenade' here).

SET FREE YOUR FLOW

Equally beware, however, of the American boys who will tell you that you are 'an independent individual capable of making your own decisions...' (true), and that you '...should enjoy being young with rampantly free sexual exploration' (not so true). Being a woman is a beautiful blessing in many ways, yes, but this does not mean that you must be a 'gift' for many (most who will prove to be undeserving) at the expense of your own dignity and the gradual degradation of your soul in the process.

Finally, you'll realize it's only when you've let go of a dependence on someone that a more genuine connection between the two of you actually develops. When you can pray for their happiness, even if this has to occur without you or your current status quo. Human beings inherently value genuineness and kindness more than any other qualities.

Dear *yıldız çiçeğim* ('star flower') ... My Dalya.

May you hopefully be able to discover your calling earlier on in life- enough to focus more intensely on one or two interests that can lead to a lifetime of both professional success as well as personal fulfilment. Elders tell us not to place 'all our eggs' into 'one basket'. That is real, but remember: so is suffering from a lifetime of indecision and vacillating between various options.

A CENTERED VIEW

May you figure out early on how to differentiate between your ego and self-preservation. When you react negatively to something, ask yourself: is it instinctual protection, or at times natural-occurring human selfishness? If it's the latter, like one of the poems in my first poetry book says, *"Tame your ego, not your hopes"*. You could very well be hoping for more attention from someone, for instance: yet someone's genuine and momentary focus on their work or other people in their lives may not always mean they don't value you in your own special way. Including overworking mommy, who apologizes for all the times she's been glued to her laptop- writing away- when you'd been craving more play time =)

I could not always love you perfectly, or have been able to express it as often as you deserved (not just for being my daughter, but for being the amazingly kind human you are in general) but believe me: I've always loved you whole-heartedly.

Your *'momma cici'**

* ('sweet' mommy in Turk-lish. Half Turkish, Half English. Your first words were bi-culturally dichotomous as well. Coincidence? I think not)

When You Become What You've Read About: the Atypical Mama and Papa Bears

When my house was raided by police after my husband was politically imprisoned and I was left alone with a 7-month-old baby in my hands- I put on a smiling face despite my rapid heartbeat, and even offered them tea. Putting on appearances of being 'okay', even whilst crying inside, was in my blood after all.

When a preordered cake was on my table- two days after July 15th, and invitations and party favor gifts had already been prepared; I gave them out to the would-be-attendees anyway after each event-cancellation phone call. I took pictures with my daughter- so she could have that memory immortalized (if she ever develops into a nostalgic/ photography-loving teenager as her mommy was).

When the wife of the admiral, who had just been posing for pictures while holding our baby mere weeks ago, suddenly didn't have anything to say on the phone in response to me crying to her. "My husband would never betray his country! There's got to have been a mistake." She remained silent.

When you're prevented from boarding your flight back to the United States after paying a visit to your politically-imprisoned husband to show him your baby daughter, and everyone looks at you like a criminal as you're escorted to the police area to discuss your surprising, uncompensated 'travel ban' and flight cancellations (and have to from thenceforth continuously frequent police stations for paperwork and legal requests).

When you've faced all of the above and countless other similarly movie-like, dramatic moments: your life flashes before your eyes like a television series, and you can only hope for the quintessentially-Hollywood 'happy ending' of justice and reunion.

I've already mentioned, dear reader, the irony I feel in my having studied politics in college and graduate school, only to later become a victim of it rather than a professional politician. My husband himself was also a 'student of politics' in a way, I suppose. As a naval officer who had to attend military school- often on campus and away from his family- since the age of 13, he had to study a lot about domestic and global politics in order to be able to best 'defend' the country in case of an attack.

Could he ever have foreseen that such an 'attack' would be an internal one? Not only at the state level, but professional backstabbing by his own military colleagues whom he'd seen as 'friends', while they'd apparently been viewing him as 'competition' to get rid of through unproveable slander?

I'd known politics, dear reader, but not a single thing

about 'the military' until I met Kemal in 2009. He'd worn all white to our coffee date- 'Ak' in color (*white*), coincidentally like his conscience of any 'wrongdoing' that'd warrant any type of arrest (alluding here to my YouTube documentary on the events, entitled 'Alnım Ak').

Cut to: Summer of 2011. By that point we'd grown closer than 'just friends', and I'd told my mother he was serious about me. I remember sunbathing on one of the Princess' Islands off of Istanbul with her, and the newspaper headline was about the imprisonment of then General İlker Başbuğ. The phone rang just then, and it was Kemal: a military officer, and my mother's Spidey-sense tingled. "Be careful," she began. "Look at these headlines arresting military officers. What if you marry him and they arrest him too? It's a dangerous occupation."

"I doubt it, mom," I'd always say. "Kemal has an 'Atatürkçü' lifestyle and ideals simultaneous with his religious faith. The government will like a multi-faceted soldier like him."

How naïve I was. My husband was never a member of the Gülenist organization. No substantial 'FETO' evidence was ever found on him anyway, and it was never the reason given for his imprisonment. Kemal was imprisoned, rather, for being 'in the middle'.

One of his closest so-called friends, in fact (a man whose wife had befriended me in the last port-town we'd been stationed

A CENTERED VIEW

in before his arrest- Foça- and told me our baby daughters would 'play and grow up together') not only didn't defend him, but actually testified that Kemal had remained 'suspiciously neutral' during the evening of the coup attempt (That's right: picture Sweden facing sanctions for its neutrality during the world war).

From what I know of Kemal, he's someone who's always wanted to please everyone. To make sure all our guests at home, or both sides of our families, were always satisfied and treated equally with respect and gifts, etc. If he bought his mother a bag, he'd want to buy my mother one too. If we ended up going out drinking one night, he'd also want to make sure he'd fulfill his Islamic obligations of fasting and giving alms. He was both 'West' and 'East' as well- albeit in a different way from myself. His unwillingness to 'choose' one side over the other, however, tragically cost him his freedom in a nation and profession that always forces one to choose.

When we were dating and sightseeing around touristic spots in Istanbul, for instance, Kemal had once stopped me from taking a selfie of us in front of the popular Blue Mosque. He'd cited that as someone in the military, if someone saw him posing in photos with 'religious symbols'- it could cost him his position. Such severity in misapplied forms of 'secularism' have unfortunately caused the reactionary, misapplied form of 'democracy' in modern Turkey; where those in power, purely because they were elected, feel they can imprison innocent people based on hearsay 'opposition' and weak 'evidence'.

Are you a man who drinks? You must automatically be a 'bad Muslim'. Why people can become so concerned with others' 'sins' (as long as they're not hurtful) if they're not the ones who will be 'burning in hellfire', as they believe, for their 'wrong-doings' (though God is also written as the *great forgiver*) is beyond me. Are you a woman who likes to dress conservatively and cover her hair? You must automatically devalue higher education and prefer being a docile wife to your husband with 'at least three kids' (as Erdoğan advocates). You don't support Erdoğan ? You must automatically support 'FETO' and deserve being labeled a 'terrorist'- being purged from your job or imprisoned, with a severity that does not allow being able to be close to your spouse and children once again in privacy.

I've already spoken at length about myself and what I've faced since 2016, dear reader. I would like to now give the remainder of this Section to my husband, Kemal. A voice from inside the political bars of Turkey. The most patriotic and law-abiding man I've ever met, who would even feel 'bad' for taking extra napkins from a restaurant. A man who hasn't been able to see his baby daughter grow up or be there for any of her birthdays or milestones. A man who, nonetheless, has supported my being here in the United States with my family for the safety and future of our daughter and family unit as a whole, since we had this blessed dual citizenship opportunity that many dream of.

I now give my 'ink' over to Kemal Akın, the 'captain' of my poems. A student and victim of politics himself. A dichotomous struggler. A decent man who, along with countless other innocently-imprisoned people like him, will one day leave those bars with their dignities in tact and heads held up high. Before I do so, I will include some personal poetry relevant to this sub-section.

I hope Kemal gets to read this collection, too, where he is, just as he's supportively done so with *The Catalyst* and *Write Out Your Drops*. In the next sub-section with his name, I'm including poetry he's written from prison to his daughter, as well as an essay he wrote specifically for this collection (encouraged by myself over the weekly telephone call I had to stay up until 4 am for, since he is not allowed to call at will).

I wanted to be his voice- both of the personal ramifications of this injustice to be on record for the world, and for his daughter to treasure as a keepsake in printed form. He is one of many- and I wish I could be able to give a voice to many such victims. I figure, if Kemal is innocent (as I know in my

SET FREE YOUR FLOW

heart, as well as looking at the particulars of his case, he is), though I don't know many of the others' specific cases: the odds are high that they are filled with innocents as well. Kemal and I feel grateful even just to be alive, as many have even lost spouses during these historic years. I cannot print each wronged voice (especially since those in Turkey are afraid to speak out, understandably so). But with Kemal's own *drop*- just one- I hope they can know that their suffering will have created a river already. Hopefully they can all *flow* into the global oceans and be free to roam the world as dignified citizens soon enough.

a newly-arrived immigrant girl
self-taught in her accented English
filling her loneliness with academic ambition
has managed to rise to the top 3
in her 4th grade Spelling Bee
...wanted to prove herself: as her own competition
she's spelled the word correctly
she's sure- the boy next to her spells the same word in the same way
he wins, while she's eliminated
in shock, she remains quiet, but jaded
'...they must have misheard through my accent'
since then, few people have understood things she's meant
the outcome: not just, and not fair
she'd won that spelling bee: fair and square
Injustice has always catalyzed her
she fights now against others that occur
helping ease the pain others too may incur

A CENTERED VIEW

THE CATALYZING SCORPION

the scavenger hunt for belonging
led her to Stavanger, among modern Vikings
her parental-caused avoidance of Scorpios halted when she married one
he'd glued her when she'd come undone: by the scorpion, she was stung
we can ultimately attract, what we purposely ignore
we can foolishly think: there will be more
only to end up catalyzed by the one
we'd once deemed a 'bore'

'BABA'

'wherefore art thou?'
she yelled
'father, oh father

                        why when I try to get closer
                     you pull yourself farther and farther?'

'father, are you even alive?'
her offspring now cries
'I hear your voice,
but I don't know your face or touch.
are they lying to me?
I'm not being told much'

                        one was a prisoner of his ambition
                          the other- a prisoner of politics
                   both affected deeply their vulnerable nestlings
                  cross-generational pain, tugs at the heartstrings

SET FREE YOUR FLOW

KEMAL 'AK' AKIN'S Ode to the 'Little Mermaid'

Dalya is a very lovely girl
She's our diamond
and she's our pearl
Since you've been
away
My head is in a painful whirl

You're our life's miracle
Rainbows have pink, orange,
and purple
I yearn to see them reflect in
your eyes' twinkle

In our nest,
I'm dreaming of D sleeping on
her daddy's chest

All this mess will come to rest
Our prayers won't go to waste

I know I'm the luckiest dad

For her happiness, I will do my
best
We'll make up for our losses in
the past
In the ocean, my ship is sailing
from east to west
Your captain can see the land
from the ship's mast
Soon, we'll get rid of the pest
Our happiness will forever last

Away from you, I'm adrift
For me,
your existence is a gift
When my ship comes to the
port
Could you please give me a lift?
Though I'm not a good poet
Our future will be marvelous, I
bet

From now on, don't be sad

A CENTERED VIEW

June 2021

My darling daughter,

How I wish I could have been able to hug you tight and say these following verses while looking into your hazel eyes in real life, rather than to the photograph of you I've attached to my magnetic cupboard here in this prison cell.

Just as our eyes locked miraculously in that moment right after you were born, how I wish I could do so every night while telling you 'goodnight', every morning while telling you 'good morning my sweet girl'. Though I can't do so, know that you are my last thought every night before I go to sleep, and my first one every morning after I open my eyes: God is my witness.

I remember a saying I'd once heard about how a father can 'sell the world in exchange for a *smile* from his daughter,' while I can only do so with the memory of yours- which I've engraved into every cell in my being. And I'm thankful even for that- and my heart and my thoughts are with you and your lovely mom, my mermaids.

I envision the moment when I can finally be free to come to you in person and hug you so tightly that it can feel almost as if time is able to stand still.

In a movie we watched here, there was a saying that fathers fight for their children and live for their promises to them- and I promise to fight for your future to the best of my ability, despite these unjust conditions. I promise you that, God-willing, everything is going to beautiful: for where there's hope, there can be miracles.

I heard from your mother than your first tooth fell- the same one I'd been the first to see appear when you were about five or six months old. It was symbolic of the tragedy that the time we've been apart is now longer than the lifetime of a tooth.

We were so excited that we wanted to throw you a little *'Diş buğdayı'* party to celebrate it, as Turkish tradition beholds. We had ordered the decorations, cake, as well as the invitations which had already gone out to the neighbors for July 17th. It was to be a Sunday, and your mother said more people could be free on that day to attend.

Remembering those days takes me back to when I couldn't stand being away from you for too long and would drop by our *'lojman'* military-housing during my lunch breaks from work, just to breathe in your heavenly smell. It pains and surprises me, thus, to think of how I've now managed to be able to be away from you for this long: 1,800 days and counting.

I thank God for giving me the strength to be able to go on despite this heavy pain- especially after knowing that that baby is now an almost six-year-old angelic child who wishes for her 'baba's return' with every shooting star, angel-number 11:11 on the clock her mom points out, every candle ever blown and every night before bed.

My dearest one. You were only about seven-months-old when they separated us, leaving you fatherless and your mother husbandless. You hadn't even begun to crawl yet- I can still remember your efforts to do so on your stomach as you laid on the carpet.

In the first 3 months of our separation, they didn't even allow me to have any picture of you, let alone any prison visits. The first time I was allowed to finally see you was through the picture of you your mom thought of to print on an allowed t-shirt to send in to me. And yet, I had been waiting a very long time to finally meet you, my child- 44 years, in fact, to become a father. Even a picture of you had been deemed too much by them.

I couldn't witness anything. Not your tooth party, your first or any subsequent birthday parties, your first time crawling and later taking your first steps, your first sentences, your first songs. I couldn't see your beautiful face and hear your angelic voice for years. I couldn't hold your hand as you walked to school, when you received your first diploma as a preschooler, when you first did your homework or drew your first pictures (I'm sure you wouldn't like my own drawings too much).

I couldn't prepare toast to send you off to school, and later pick you up from school- proudly witnessing you pointing me out to your friends as 'my dad'.

I couldn't be there to embrace you when you were sick or sad- when you needed both of your parents. I couldn't help to brush your hair or calm you when you were afraid of thunder. I couldn't take you to the park and point you out proudly as 'my daughter'.

I couldn't be there to teach you how to ride a bicycle, fly a kite, or run in the fields.

SET FREE YOUR FLOW

We've also missed the seasons, darling daughter. We couldn't watch falling snow together, couldn't throw snowballs to one another, or go sledding. I couldn't warm your fingers cold from the snow with my breath.

We couldn't smell spring's first flowers together, couldn't chase butterflies together, couldn't roll in the grass or share excitement over rainbows. In the summer, we couldn't make sandcastles, go swimming, or make wishes on shooting stars together. We couldn't walk on the crunchy leaves of autumn together or enjoy beautiful foliage views in our mutual birthday month of November.

I couldn't, with the responsibility of a father, teach you about life and spirituality- our faith, religious holidays, morality and our prayers.

We couldn't watch cartoons or go to the movies together. I couldn't play your favorite game of 'Hide-and-Seek' with you or witness you performing the steps you learned in your ballet classes and school/summer shows.

We couldn't celebrate Mother's and Father's Day together- couldn't get a gift for your mom doing both parenting jobs together, or for your grandma and grandpa there in the US who've sacrificed so much for all of us during this difficult time.

I couldn't share your various joys and excitements, encourage you during your hesitations, guide you when you needed courage and ease your concerns.

I couldn't be your childhood 'hero'. I couldn't be an actual father for you. What would otherwise be daily, 'routine' things for many fathers and their children are for us now so monumental- because we were not allowed to experience them.

I tried to find consolation in your pictures and drawings for me- sometimes falling asleep with them in my hand. Because of the terrible timing of my allotted family-call-time due to our geographical time difference, I couldn't even hear your speak to me for years: never live, anyway, just through recorded little message clips your mom would play for me.

"I drew cats for you, baba. Will you come to my birthday party?" I still get a lump in my throat each time I recall your voice in such messages. And, of course, "I love you, baba."

I couldn't do anything for you and your mom from here. My physical inability to be there for you handicapped me from this prison and I did what I could do- pray for you and dream about a beautiful future together. I never, ever lost my hope or vision. Even though I only had mere and brief memories to hang on to.

Those moments when we were finally able to get you to fall asleep as a baby, when we played on the bed while mommy was busy and I lifted you up in my arms and said 'let's fly to….'and you giggled each time I named various cities around the world as I lifted you. I remember the stressful times (I regret now being too much of a worrywart over things like water temperature) of bath time, your lovely babble when we first went in the sea together and you were able to sit up on the sandy shore. When I proudly carried you on my chest around town in a baby carrier.

Every day, through my brief, caged view of the sky: I tell airplanes, clouds and seagulls to always carry my '*selam*' and my love-filled greetings to you, my darling daughter with a heart as beautiful as she is.

As a part of our faith, *babacım,* know that we will be rewarded for this injustice and we will make up for these days to the best of our abilities. The vision of you- and my innocence- keeps me standing and enables me to go on living. You have to believe too, *babacım*. During this roughest time in my life, I have learned the value of being grateful for everyone and every little joy in one's daily life, as well as of being patient.

I learned that, even if you are right, it is never worth it to hurt the heart of someone you love. As I read here in 'Don Coyote' (I hope to read it with you soon), we always have a lot of friends in our 'good days' who can suddenly leave us alone when the weather gets cloudy. I realized how I had collected such friends and relatives over the years, who've shown their true colors during this time by not extending their support to us. This reminds me of another saying, one by Martin Luther King Jr: *the ultimate measure of a man is not where he stands in moments of comfort but where he stands at times of challenge and controversy.* We will hopefully evaluate such 'unnecessary' fair-weather acquaintances in our new lives after this nightmare ends.

I've learned and felt to my very core the immense magnitude of everyday joys that the average person going through their daily lives can take for granted: walking and sitting on grass, watching the sun rise and set, walking on the beach or taking a boat ride while inhaling the sea, listening to the sounds of the birds and trees, taking long walks in all kinds of weather without doing anything else but simply strolling along, lying on the knees of someone you love or on the sand together, driving accompanied to music, buying gifts for those you care about, being able to look someone in the eyes and telling them you love them, dancing to a song you love together, being able to watch your favorite shows whenever you want, sleeping in a quiet and peaceful environment without the snoring sounds of a dozen other people with you, and countless others.

Babacım, I call my world here, the world of 'small forms of happiness'. And because we're not allowed much in our prison cells (not even scissors/glue, so I have to cut out cartoons and designs for you from newspapers to add to my letters through the use of a nail clipper and chewing gum) we've come to truly appreciate joys from even the smallest things and to not take anything for granted. To not waste anything in extravagance, not even toilet paper. Most of all- to appreciate the joy upon hearing even routine 'good news' from loved ones' lives outside of here. When we manage to have a decent meal to eat, when we're able to get hot water for a warm shower, a rare occasion where we don't have to wait a long time for using the bathroom, being able to have an unshared bed of our own to sleep on, etc.

But my darling daughter- most of all I've come to appreciate what I still have in you and for our health. For I've met people here far less fortunate. I've met men who never even got to see their children being born, men who lost their loved ones while they were locked up, men who went through divorces and the pain of finding out their children and wives got cancer, men whose family members too are jailed, and even those who don't even have anyone to call or write to them.

My little mermaid. I couldn't be there for your mommy mermaid- who I found in the rough oceans- when she had to be both a father and mother to you, when she had to handle so many things (with both the bad days and good days) for which I couldn't accompany her (including having her book publishing dreams coming true). I never got to tell her everything I realized the value of more now that I've been here, and tell her in her eyes that my love and appreciation for her only grew more each day. But you are both in my dreams and prayers every morning and night, and I know that rainbows will appear at the end of this storm. I thank God every day for having experienced both of you in my life- for you having been the peak of my life's happiness in my memories.

My Dalya: when you were born, life and all the flowers in it grew more colorful, the sun shone brighter, my world grew lovelier and everything took on more meaning. Please never forget this: for me, one smile from you is worth a lifetime.

My smart, sensitive and kind daughter. From what you've been told (for your young psychology), you knew your dad to be 'a captain on a long ship voyage'- and I actually have come to feel that way too, along with you. I feel in my heart this ship is finally nearing the harbor and, when it does, I will hug you both very tightly and never let go in our new life together.

The apple of my eye, sweetest part of my soul, my heartbeat: they say life is what we make of the challenges we're faced with. Life is also said to be 'trouble' while only death is not. But we must not grow gloomy and lose hope that our story will have a happy ending, no matter what hand we've been dealt so far. What doesn't kill us truly can make us stronger, and I believe with all my heart that at the end of this arduous path we will all triumph and prevail. I know in my heart we will be able to laugh about these days one day, and this forced, political separation too will come to an end.

We will sing, dance, fly kites, ride bikes, and travel together; just like the way I'd lift you up in the air as a baby and say 'let's go to...' and list various places…only this time, we'll actually go to them.

I will do my best always to be there for you through both your joyful as well as saddest moments, and will only continue to be proud of you always.

My mermaids- you are my prayers and dreams having have come true in this lifetime and I am always grateful. I am comforted knowing that God is watching you both- *Allaha emanetsiniz.*

I wish I could hang on to the wind, jump on a cloud, and come beside you…I wish I could frequent you through a butterfly in your garden…wave 'hello' at my little mermaid in the form of a lightning bolt through her bedroom window.

Grateful to have a daughter I adore
Every day I only miss you more and more

Our precious- I promise you, all the truth will one day come to light
I will then spend the rest of my days as my Princess' Knight

SET FREE YOUR FLOW

My Dalya, you are the prettiest flower
How marvelous to have you as my daughter

Nothing can compare to being your father
Longing for time spent together,
Know your daddy will be loving you forever

With love always,
your 'captain' baba

Dear reader. It is impossible for me (Selin) to speak on behalf of all the political prisoners of Turkey since the 2016 coup attempt. I have no idea what their 'crimes' and case folders consist of. I particularly cannot fathom, for instance, how mothers imprisoned (some with their children) could possibly be so dangerous to the 'state'- especially at a time in Turkey when many actual criminals and murderers of women have controversially been released.

There are just so many stories. Stories like the 45-year-old wife and mother who succumbed to cancer and ultimately death after her military pilot officer husband was imprisoned- and he couldn't attend her funeral even handcuffed due to 'coronavirus restrictions'. I was told by Kemal that he was since able to briefly visit their two surviving children for a couple of hours, before being taken back to the prison for solitary confinement to 'quarantine' for 2 weeks. I can't even imagine what that man must have been running through his head during those additional 2 weeks of isolated torture after such a tragedy.

As I've said: I can only be a voice for one 'drop'- Kemal- and vicariously through him, all the innocently-imprisoned ones like him. The man who'd once responded to someone over dinner (after the person had casually and jokingly said *'you guys are the military- you can always do a coup and get rid of leaders if things get bad in Turkey'*): "Military coups have always taken this country backwards- don't even joke of such a thing". A man whose only 'crime' on that night of July 15th was choosing his professional duty (befitting his high rank) to stay in his office to guard the premises until the morning (when they took him in) instead of saying "*…to hell with this: I'm going back home to my wife and baby daughter*".

A man whom I know was raised by dichotomous struggles of the *traditional* and the *liberal* of his own. A man who was the traditional 'Paul' to my liberal 'Kaitlin' in *The Catalyst*. A man I'm sure is crimsoning as he (hopefully) reads these lines too, as he told me he'd blushed while reading the novel. If so? *Sorry, honey. But what can I say? I write freely. It's our true story, and it can hopefully help to inspire others. You did choose to marry an outspoken and American-raised feminist, after all :)*

SET FREE YOUR FLOW

THE REBUILDER

there's a guest in the garden:
a bumble bee,
buzzing intensely
searching
beautifully chubby,
circling
forages around wildly
(I'm pretty sure it's a *she*)
in and out of the remaining twigs
dashing about repeatedly
in frustration

a mother scorned,
we hypothesize
in exasperation

her nest is now gone
following the landscaping
she's relentless:
her vengeance, through rebuilding

she accepts what is gone…eventually

whether the first disappointment, or the tenth
her pain and loss, add to her strength

WRECKAGE

words of sympathy, aiming affinity
are easy to express: kind in tone, but depth-wise empty
when you're not the one who's faced a national tragedy

one's family could have faced affliction, political displacement
and separation
disillusionment of an entire nation

another's can involve untimely death- heartbreaking catastrophe
or being fired from their livelihood- economic adversity

or perhaps immigration: causing ridiculed accents and frizzy hair
an ever-nomadic situation: never belonging here, there, or anywhere

allow the cursed to cry it out
let them express their gloom
healing away the doom

                                            freedom of speech
                                          shouldn't be deemed treason
                                          don't judge someone's words
                                      without considering their reason

empathize with facers of misfortune
keep your judgement in check
for at any given moment
your life too can become   *a wreck*

SECTIONAL ANECDOTES

Growing up bi-cultural has meant:

-Realizing everything they told you about Istanbul being 'special' was a one-sided exaggeration. It turns out, for instance, that, no: the Bosphorus is not the only lovely strait in the world (just symbolic to be situated in both Asia and Europe). And, no: it is not logical to call anyone a 'traitor' every time they critique their homeland. We can't truly be loving what we automatically approve blindly, without the acceptance of all its admitted faults.

-Western education teaching you to be inquisitive and open-minded, while 'religious' Turks claim it's 'sacrilegious' to have questions and want to do research before blind acceptance (meanwhile, critical-thinking is actually encouraged in the Koran). For example: when you call the Prophet's beloved wife until her death- Khadija- the first Islamic 'feminist' (a twice-widowed businesswoman, 15 years his senior, who also proposed to him).

- Recognition that most of the so-called 'close people' in your circle have only loved you conditionally: *"You'll be inviting them for dinner- we need them to be our friends"/ "You're going to dress appropriately, smile, and politely greet everyone- you're representing us."/"He dumped me. I'm sad. Let's meet."*

A CENTERED VIEW

Section V. Flowing Through Creating

LION IN THE CAT'S REFLECTION

EVOLVE

each time life threw me a curveball-
I learned to pitch it on my own,
and hit home runs for survival

I saw the lion in the cat's reflection
the potential
before disappointments
threatened to make that little girl believe she was unworthy
of dreaming, or of compliments

I held on to that image during the moments
when the cat couldn't even affect a mouse

hidden behind the mane

finally
I roared
I soared

A CENTERED VIEW

DESPOSING OF DESPONDENCE

vulnerability
eats away
through our shields
our skin
you hold your head high
noticing their gaze
like a freshly cut rose
showcased in a vase

only to wilt when alone
no water, light, or attention
that temporarily feel like home
words are empty promises
when merely uttered
without their definitions shown

I decide, hence, to hold on to the unreliability
and allow change to be my constant
life is rarely an offspring of excitement and safety
can't have it all, though acceptance is new layer of skin

no need to be despondent

What the Leo Mane Hides

Another lifetime 'struggle' for me (aside from the cultural, generational, and political ones I've gone into) has most certainly been: self-image. My attitude towards confidence. Those who've heard of my books through my usage of social media promotions will certainly have seen the visual-storyteller side of me: I adore poetic book trailers and voiceovers. With each photo shoot I took part in to use in such visuals and my 'Author' profiles: I had to quiet my own impostor syndrome alongside my fears over what 'people' must 'certainly be thinking' (some based on actual life experience).

"Why is a Turkish, Muslim woman posing for artistic pictures? And she's a mother. And she's not model-thin. And she's married..." That list accumulated from voices in my head- some imagined, some from memory- can go on and on. Meanwhile, how many times had I met someone hurtful 'behind the scenes'- who put on 'appearances' of being the 'ideal' friend, spouse, student, professional, devout person, while committing hurtful acts in private? As I've grown self-acceptant, if I were to be confronted by such people I'd now confidently be able to say:

"Thanks for your unsolicited opinion, but we're obviously at different frequencies. Did you experience the things

A CENTERED VIEW

I've experienced? Have you faced the same situations I've faced, and in my shoes? No. My daughter is proud of me. My family is proud of me. I am proud of me. You should be proud of you, and mind your own business..."

However, I believe I'm now also 'centered' and aware enough to the fact that I even have such self-accepting (yet, at their core, defensive) thoughts is precisely because of all the dichotomous Turkish-American struggles I've written about here.

Many American friends would tell me throughout the years, the now cliché: *"Who cares what they think? It's your life, and you're not hurting anyone!"* The Turks care. Especially the bi-cultural ones. They care. For various reasons, but they care. Regardless of their particular reasons, they mainly care because they have the inherent need to compare.

Have you gotten a better job than them? A showier partner or spouse? A better house? A better car? A later version of the 'it' smartphone of the year? The list goes on and on, only with this addendum: *how has it been received by our circle? Has his/ her new* (*insert name of positive development in life here*) *gotten him/her more likes? More followers? More friends? More customers? More sales?* You become their experiment. Their litmus test. *"If he/she's done it, and it's been accepted, I can do it, too. Maybe even better"*.

SET FREE YOUR FLOW

If you have tried, and you haven't had success? The same people can be one of the first ones, unfortunately, to cast the 'stone'; as if they hadn't been the one to secretly wish to try the same. That is why, I've come to accept the unreliability in life, while still maintaining the Turkish/Muslim part at the core of my identity that believes in '*hayırlısı* (for the best)'.

I don't necessarily believe in- however- the Turkish adage on '*kismet*', or, pre-destined fate. In my humble, and dichotomous, Turkish-American opinion: I believe God and the Universe present certain (yes, predetermined) options in our paths, yet after a certain age it is up to our own free-will and choices that determines which path we go on to experience in life. After all, without free-will: where would the celestial test of our spiritual faith be? Nonetheless, despite our at times mistaken choices, I always try my best to maintain the belief that God is on our side; like the ideal parent who may disapprove, but always loves.

that offer you'd been counting on-
wasn't truly a lifetime gem, like you'd sought
heed the Creator's warning-
they weren't for you, despite what you may have thought
accept your exception
believe in redirection
reject undeserved rejection

A CENTERED VIEW

'Art Doesn't Pay'

Art. Why art? Why *not* art? I believe creativity to be a human need: for variety, for purpose, for sanity, for beauty, for hope.

Creativity exists inside all of us. Even if, dear reader, you've never picked up a pen to write or draw, or held a microphone or instrument to create music- you employ creativity more than you realize.

God, too, is *creative*, after all. One only has to gaze at the stars and look at the meticulous plan and symmetrical beauty of nature and the seasons all around us. So, too, are we as His creations.

When you're cooking soup and you want to 'mix it up' that week to try something a little differently, with a novel ingredient? You're *creative*. When you're washing your car or mowing the lawn and do so whistling a tune to make the routine go faster? You're *creative.* When you're signing your name somewhere and you want to use a special pen because it will 'look nicer'? That's right. You're *creative*.

Yet- as with money or a joyful life- creativity, too, can sometimes be conditioned and instilled in us as something 'shameful' or 'excessive' among some circles. As if a largely ascetic life, deprived of pleasure, could somehow by itself make one 'moral' and heaven-worthy; without regarding the irony of why the loving God we believe in would want us to refrain from joy in life, only to prepare us for an afterlife in which we are promised to be able to do so.

Growing up among my two cultures has meant the desire to create art, but not knowing how much of your soul you can 'set free' without your family feeling 'shamed'. You're told, in fact, it isn't even 'relevant' to set your soul free with *art* in order to cure boredom and purposelessness. That it's a waste of time that could be spent on other 'more valuable' things, like baking spinach pies or dusting the house décor- shining yet more things meant to appease others rather than your own self.

But I've written this collection, dear reader, to take that chance. To take that risk. So that if there is ever a young child- or soul young at heart- reading these verses somehow and they are going through a similar inner struggle, they can know that it can be done. It can, and perhaps even *must* be done.

I sincerely hope from the bottom of my heart and very soul that you've been enjoying my musings, dear reader. But, no matter what. As I sit here typing these last lines, I can attest it sure feels damn good for me to have expressed them. To have gotten it out 'there', wherever 'there' may have been. ('Getting it out' of people- to appease their psyches and souls by talking out their issues- is one of the main functions, after all, of a psychotherapist as well, isn't it?)

For most of us- especially independent ('indie') ones not represented by a well-known publish company or agent- art may not pay much in dollars. But it surely does so in life-purpose identification and spiritual satisfaction. We persist not to be done favors (the social-media prominent 'like for a like' or 'review for a review', for example) but be given an equal chance to share our art- the quality of which we believe in. To start out on equal footing as the institutionalized, establishment-represented artists.

We believe in the fruit of our sacrifice and labor, which simply couldn't wait any further and needed to be birthed without the hierarchy of the literary world. We have a story, a message, a beacon of inspiration that's been brewing inside of us so poignantly that it's palpable enough to hurt when not birthed. A beacon of hope for at least someone out there who needs precisely to hear our tale at a particular time. Our art can come at a time where it may be the only way some messages- otherwise curtailed by politics or socio-cultural limitations, could be gotten across. Our art, then, becomes a bridge. A messenger of healing- of telling others "…you are not alone, fellow drop in the ocean."

Dear reader. I mentioned my newfound empathy with a large group of new women around the world- namely, prison wives. I've experienced the humiliation of being searched down to your underwear during each visit, including your toddler daughter's diaper. I know the pain of being on the other side of that glass, talking to a prisoner via a now ancient-looking telephone receiver. I know the pain of not knowing what to write in their long-awaited letter from you. Shared experiences make women allies- if not quite friends- as I've mentioned before. With this experience more women have a friend in me than perhaps they even know, and vice versa. Friends are, after all, said to simply be strangers we haven't met yet.

Let's take a certain fellow instructor at one of the colleges I work at, for instance. Eileen Merwin. We were virtually introduced during the pandemic by our supervisor as fellow authors, for a school event. Yet the moment I heard that her partner was once wrongfully-incarcerated right here in the US for many years- in a realm, we were allies for life, if not yet friends since we hadn't met in person yet. She bought my book and I hers- and we genuinely enjoyed each other's work (genuineness is something no one can fake) and provided feedback. Our art had become cathartic for not only both of us-but for our loved ones as well. Her partner now lives with her and is free- I'm manifesting the same hopefully for my husband, of course. He's an artist with various paintings that she said helped him hold on to life while in prison, and she herself helped to write a theatrical sketch, in fact, about the prison experience.

Was it 'coincidence' that I'd met another partner of a wrongfully-imprisoned man, who was also both an author and an instructor at the same college where I work? Had I subconsciously wanted to feel a bit less alone in my 'unique' status- and attracted such a meeting?

There's been an undeniably increasing 'manifestation' trend lately. YouTubers are going viral through various 'Law of Attraction' videos giving advice on how to attract abundance and happiness into your life through affirmative thinking. Many times, such manifesting includes gratitude to the 'universe' for allowing the manifester's dreams to come to being, and this term also tends to vary from 'ancestors' and 'angels' and 'mother nature' and- finally, and in my view, above all- God.

Prayers to God in general have now become trendy under this overall 'manifestation' trend. Yet it is not the only way in which I feel the 'traditional' has become 'trendy' again with the 'current'. I had conversations with Turkish-American friends about how, in fact, yoga, in some ways, was similar to the Islamic daily prayers: physical movements varying between prostrating on the ground and standing up with different arm positions, for instance. 'Meditation' being akin to 'prayers' in a sense. In a way, with such open-minded thinking- we'd exemplified a cultural synthesis, so to speak. A 'gray' hypothesis from the middle of two different spiritual practices- finding synergic commonalities to both. After all, whatever we believe or don't- we are all a part of this world. A part of this universe. What I call God/Allah- you may choose to call something else. But we all have our humanity in common.

the universe flows through you, as a vessel with a creation
when you are its storyteller- you can catalyze folks into action
heed to the call, to the flow, and the Universe will thank you
with your contentment

Dear reader. I've never enjoyed the company of narrow-minded people: people who practice one-way thinking without consideration for any alternative opinions or possibilities. I don't always agree with 'new age' folks- to be honest- and believe in some things more conservatively than they do. But that's the rare

A CENTERED VIEW

beauty of my dichotomy: I may not agree with them, but because I've grown up facing lifestyle choices from both liberal and conservative expectations- I don't, and cannot, judge them.

Spending your time and energy on art just for the joy of living and breathing that art- being in the flow of the creative process through which your soul feels most *purpose*... is enigmatic to people in our lives with such closed visions. Not only can they never fathom 'the point' vis-à-vis the lack of immediate or routine/ 'paycheck style' financial rewards, they also can't comprehend an alternative purpose of 'success' when it doesn't come in a form they associate with that word. Your books aren't bestsellers? They'll assume they're 'not on par' to those that are- not gripping the powers often of publicity and the right connections for some to achieve such statuses. Your songs aren't on the radio? Same... Your paintings aren't displayed at a trendy place? Ditto...Little do they know: just one person appreciating our art sincerely is worth an eternity of strenuous labor for it.

Write Out Your Drops AND Set Free Your Flow

I've written extensively on contributing our unique stories and experiences artistically onto the world 'stage' of collective/human 'oceans'- where we could all learn from one another and feel less lonely in our individual struggles in life. In this collection- I've taken it one step further in suggesting that our cultural identity and various struggles we may have faced in them by nature (both genetic and environmental) precisely provides us with a unique imprint in our fluid souls. One that we need to take a step back and listen to once in a while, despite the rising sound of technology and globalization pressures.

Our eccentricities can become what ultimately attracts people to us the most, and the inner struggles we face in blossoming our culturally-influenced personalities can ultimately provide clues to our missions on earth. I've been attempting to bring forth a voice to injustice through creativity- making, literally, 'art' out of activism through love and not 'war'. No derogatory insults hurled at political figures- no matter how much some may deserve it, it'd achieve nothing.

I also have a deepfelt connection and love toward the land of my birth, despite my cultural and political heartbreak. I miss eating *simit* on the ferry boats of Istanbul. I miss the Aegean coast- where Dalya first experienced the sea. And I miss waking up every morning to the mystifying call of *ezan*. I realized I could not turn my back on my Turkish-American pride simply because the Türkiye-half had currently (socio-politically) turned its back on me and my core family.

> "Writing makes me feel more relevant as a human being- to connect my one drop of contribution to the entire ocean of humanity in the world..."

The quote above is included in a section on my website entitled 'Author's Writing Process'- taken from one of my first literary interviews. In it I highlight how- once I'd taught myself English- I enjoyed taking it one step further and combining my love of words with my love of music: namely through writing 'lyrics' to 'melodies' I'd create in my head. These later became poems to describe moments in my life. Simply writing daily journal notes or 'dear diary' entries wouldn't satisfy my need for creativity after some point, and over the years, my academic research writing didn't satisfy my soul either. (I wish, in retrospect, I would have majored in English Literature or something of that sort). I wanted to take a brief excerpt from the interview, for I believe it sums up my artistic 'flow' perfectly for the sake of this collection:

SET FREE YOUR FLOW

"…As an only child, I remember having had an overactive imagination, sometimes even pretending to be 'interviewed' on the radio about some book series (!) I'd had. I've always been a pondering wonderer, preferring to reflect on my thoughts alone rather than feel lost in noisy crowds. Hence, writing in general has always felt both natural and like 'home' for me…Like the female lead in the novel, I too had to initially cope with becoming a 'bored housewife' immediately into my marriage- as I also had to relocate to a foreign land and grapple with solitude, like Kaitlin Maverick. Despite the beauty of Stavanger, Norway, the slower tempo of life (in comparison to my native NYC) was difficult for me to adapt to- especially as, I later realized, I'd always idealized a marriage or live-in relationship to be full of more 'romantic adventures' than domestic docility.

I refused to allow myself into a depression, however, and knew my need for productivity to maintain my self-esteem; hence, the 'catalyst' for my starting to work on my lifelong dream of writing a novel began…In the 7-8 years in total it took me to complete the novel: life happened. I was a military wife in Norway and the novel took a halt at various points due to relocating, my pregnancy, my husband's politically-motivated (sans any 'criminal' action or evidence) incarceration in Turkey, and my moving back to my childhood home in NYC to adjust to a new life with my parents and my toddler daughter (in that order). I also knew I had to make ends meet, and so took on a lot of classes teaching international students.

After all of the struggles I went through raising my daughter, I felt like maybe everything had happened so that I could finally release it when I was more ready to- at the 'right' time. It wasn't easy- and the story had to be edited and re-edited about 3 times before it could be published (and during a rough time too at that, with COVID-19). I still believe in my story so much, however, and believe everything truly does happen for a reason. I know somehow- perhaps slowly but surely- this cumulation of my hard-work and sleepless hours will reach the right hands at the right time and 'catalyze' whoever needs to read a story like 'The Catalyst' at this particular time in history…"

Writing makes us all legendary. All of our experiences- no matter how seemingly trivial, controversial, or even grand and dramatic- through writing them out, will have a purpose…. To be able to affect, and perhaps even catalyze…through our verses, even long after our bodies are gone…

SET FREE YOUR FLOW

THE PAIN OF FREE WILL

I simply want to express
my current state of distress
I can't have it all
we must admit when we fall
I can't triumph professionally
and feel happy emotionally
I can't be the perfect mother
and also make time for another
I can't maintain my socio-cultural duties
and also prioritize my wants and needs
sometimes
I can't be both the East and the West
and I wish I had a compass
that could decide for me

less stress

LIONESS

they hunt for the kill
whilst you do to defend
and survive
you're not the darkness of their hatred
let them eat themselves up while
you thrive
you affect beyond what meets the eye
delicately strong butterfly
you are feared, yet tireless

worn but mighty, dear lioness

A CENTERED VIEW

IGNITERS

summer nights
and summer days
facing sunsets
in a haze
our lives have become a maze
pain we mistake for excitement
who can share our atonement?
lighten our burdens
exorcise our demons
we had set their souls ablaze
we were never a passing phase
being without our deep love of legends
is their punishment
they can live out their days, faking fulfillment

THE MASTER'S MUSE

the lady's broken smile,
curved higher after she'd left this earth
her absence added to her now legendary worth

didn't anyone tell her, back then?
maybe she was never broken
she never had to suppress fully-expressed joy, words unspoken

we only seem flawed to hearts of a different style
we will be shown effort by the true ones worth the while

AFTERWORD

As the founder of the creative term 'flow', psychologist Mihaly Csikszentmihalyi would hopefully agree with me when I say the following: I've been bleeding out my art and writing out my drops. And, with my writing: setting free the natural *flow* of my bicultural soul despite socio-cultural 'taboos' and hindrances.

I've been doing purely so for the sake of doing so; not to obtain some end result that is out of my control. The only thing I can control is my conscious concentration on my art, which gives me joy during otherwise difficult times. The art of storytelling- both autobiographical here and fantastical with my fiction novels- merely for my joy in the creation of it. To be able to joyfully create art out of having been collateral damage of dichotomous social pressures- as well as much drama in life overall- provides me a sense of fairness and healing.

Regardless of how pessimistic my outlook may have appeared in this collection about my duality- to be crystal clear: I am now wholly acceptant and even celebratory of it. I love being an offspring of the cultural legacy of the Ottoman Empire, as well as forebearer of the secular (which I do not believe was ever intended to be anti-religion), socio-

A CENTERED VIEW

intellectual remnants of the world-renowned Atatürk. His lingering resonance among the youth of Turkey- despite all the politics of the past decade- fills me with hope that my birth country will, too, somehow be able to recover from its dichotomous neuroses, and come out of everything much stronger. United. Not divided.

I love having experienced first-hand the value of true democracy and freedom in the United States- more palpable since my 2017 return here after my airport trauma in Turkey.

I love being able to connect with the great variety of beautiful music in Turkey (often beautiful dichotomous fusions themselves), where reggaeton/pop sounds can be found intertwined with belly-dance rhythms and Turkish instruments like *ney* and *saz*.

Following my nearly decade-long process publishing *The Catalyst*; I see now it's truly been a 'catalyst' for me as well in its own right. Not only has it improved my writing ability, it has also given me a fulfilling sense of purpose: enjoying the cathartic process and encouraging others to do the same, rather than writing to employ some mission solely for sales or entertainment.

Regardless of whether your path involves art or not, I know it will somehow involve innovative thinking and creativity- cornerstones in nearly any profession imaginable on this earth, in one form or another. I've discovered my motivation and purpose. I can only hope I have been able to help you get at least one step closer to discovering yours. *Let my storytelling be your 'catalyst' to release your 'flow' and your 'flood of drops'...*

Selin

SET FREE YOUR FLOW

like the tides of the mighty oceans
receding before flooding the shores,
rivers catapulting into rapids and waterfalls

you too have a *flow*
an inherent inclination of which way to go
Mother Nature must outpour when it feels that call:
just as your own essence- the one of your very soul

yet the society-pressured logical mind can repress
life choices the spirit wishes to express

like wind currents harnessed into energy
forces of your duality- in unison- can create synergy

Set free your glow. Set free your **flow**

MAKE LEMONADE OUT OF LEMONS
IDIOM

storyteller

be the flower growing through the concrete
flow like a moderate breeze- no frost, no heat

ABOUT THE AUTHOR

SELIN SENOL-AKIN is an Adjunct Professor of language education, human rights activist, and a featured spoken word artist, poet, and writer.

She's read her poetry at annual NYC events like *Pynk* and the multinational *Versos Estivales Poetry Festival*, with work included in the published anthology of the same name. Her short story, 'Ordinary', was featured in the feminist anthology *Flash*. She was also chosen as a featured poet to represent the borough of Queens at the popular open-mic showcase 'Inspired Word'.

Her debut poetry collection, *Write Out Your Drops,* became a #1 Amazon New Release in the Fall of 2020. *The Catalyst,* her well-received novel first published at the onset of the pandemic, has also become a #1 release among Scandinavian literature, and its long-requested sequel, *The Penance*, will be released in 2022.

A CENTERED VIEW

a dual individual

Reader's Favorite *Five-Star Reviews*

"*Set Free Your Flow* is a must-read for people wanting to discuss the big issues faced by young immigrants but don't have the position of understanding through experience of their own. The author is frank, honest, and open…"

K.C Finn

"…Through her poetic verses and essays, Selin Senol-Akın provides readers with a rare glimpse into the lives of children of immigrant parents who find themselves torn between clashing cultures. The book opens with a poem titled 'A Centered View', which encapsulates the very essence of being raised in an immigrant family in America. It explores the conflict that lies within one's soul, a conflict that arises when contrasting views pull your psyche in opposite directions. The book follows Selin's life in contemporary America as a modern feminist with her roots in Turkey, who is fighting a brave battle against the imprisonment of her husband by an authoritarian regime…"

Pikasho Deka

"In this splendid book, (Selin Senol-Akın) explores some of the more frequent dichotomies we can find in everyday life and adds to them the characteristic of being born in one culture and raised in another. The most touching part of *Set Free Your Flow* is, in my opinion, the long letter that Senol-Akın's husband wrote to his daughter from prison, which makes this valuable book even more meaningful…"

Astrid Iustulin

www.ingramcontent.com/pod-product-compliance
Lightning Source LLC
Chambersburg PA
CBHW072010070526
44583CB00015B/1419